More Stories of Cats
AND THE
LIVES THEY TOUCH

More Stories of
Cats
AND THE
Lives They Touch

Edited by Peggy Schaefer

Ideals Publications
Nashville, Tennessee

ISBN 0-8249-4638-3

Published by Ideals Publications, a division of Guideposts
535 Metroplex Drive, Suite 250, Nashville, Tennessee 37211
www.idealsbooks.com

Copyright © 2005 by Ideals Publications

Printed and bound in the U.S.A. by RR Donnelley

Library of Congress Cataloging-in-Publication Data

More stories of cats and the lives they touch / edited by Peggy Schaefer.
    p. cm.
  ISBN 0-8249-4638-3 (alk. paper)
  1. Cats—Anecdotes. 2. Cat owners—Anecdotes. 3. Human-animal
relationships—Anecdotes. I. Schaefer, Peggy, date.
  SF445.5.M6794 2004
  636.8—dc22

                              2004025828

Publisher, Patricia A. Pingry   Assistant Editor, Melinda Rathjen
Associate Publisher, Peggy Schaefer   Copy Editors, Marie Brown,
Series Designer, Marisa Calvin   Melinda Rathjen

Front jacket photo © Rachael Hale Photography Limited 2005. All rights reserved.
Rachael Hale is a registered trademark of Rachael Hale Photography Limited.

10 9 8 7 6 5 4 3 2 1

ACKNOWLEDGMENTS

BENINGHOFF, MARY. "Mahgy" from Cat Miracles. Copyright © 2003 by Brad Steiger and Sherry Hansen Steiger.
Used by permission of Adams Media Corporation. CARAS, ROGER A. "Feline Intuition" from A Celebration of
Cats. Copyright © 1986 by Roger A. Caras. Published by Simon & Schuster. Reprinted by permission of Curtis
Brown Ltd. MARY ELLEN. "Q: Is There a God? A: Meow!" from God's Messengers. Copyright © 2003 by Allen
and Linda Anderson. Reprinted with permission of New World Library, Novato, CA. www.newworldlibrary.com.
FRANCIS, DONNA. "One Lucky Cat" from Angel Cats. Copyright © 2004 by Allen and Linda Anderson.
Reprinted by permission of New World Library, Novato, CA. FRAZIER, ANITRA with Norma Eckroate. "Clawed's
Story: The Older Cat" from It's a Cat's Life. Copyright 1985 by the authors. The Berkley Publishing Group.
GETHERS, PETER. "Meet Norton" from The Cat Who Went To Paris. Copyright © 1991 Peter Gethers. "Polite
Company" from A Cat Abroad. Copyright © 1993 by Peter Gethers. Both selections used by permission of Crown
Publishers, a division of Random House, Inc. HERRIOT, JAMES. "Olly and Ginny Settle In" from James Herriot's
Cat Stories. Copyright © 1994 by James Herriot and used by permission of St. Martin's Press, LLC in the USA
and by Harold Ober Associates, Inc. for all other territories. MCELROY, SUSAN CHERNAK. "The Angel Cat" from
Cat Caught My Heart. Copyright © 1998 by Michael Capuzzo and Teresa Banik Capuzzo. Published by Bantam
Books, Bantam Doubleday Dell Publishing Group. MCRAE, BRIAN. "Major League Assistance from 'The Sisters'"
from Angel Cats. Copyright © 2004 by Allen and Linda Anderson. Reprinted with permission of New World
Library, Novato, CA. SHEPPE, DEE. "A Cat Named Hope" from Cat Caught My Heart. Copyright © 1998 by
Michael Capuzzo and Teresa Banik Capuzzo. Bantam Books, Bantam Doubleday Dell Publishing Group, Random
House. SIMON, CLEA. "My Cat, Cyrus" from The Feline Mystique. Copyright © 2002 by Clea Simon. Used by per-
mission of St. Martin's Press. WREN, CHRISTOPHER. "Henrietta the Cat and Her Foreign Correspondent" from
The Cat Who Covered the World. Copyright © 2000 by Christopher S. Wren. Published by Simon & Schuster.

All other stories were previously published in Angels On Earth or Guideposts magazine or books. Copyright © by
Guideposts, Carmel, NY. Some material by Diane Ciarloni, Thirza Peevey, Marion Bond West, and Garnet
Hunt White used by the authors' permission.

All possible care has been taken to fully acknowledge the ownership and use of the selections in this book. If
any mistakes or omissions have occurred, they will be corrected in subsequent editions, provided notification is
sent to the publisher.

CONTENTS

For the Love

of a Cat

Feline Intuition

Roger A. Caras

One evening Jill and I were walking to a theater along West Fifty-sixth Street in Manhattan. As we passed a darkened entryway, a very plump alley cat appeared and began doing figure eights around our ankles, purring impressively. Clearly this was an act of communication. The cat was trying desperately to tell us something. We had no choice but to listen. The cat simply would not let us pass. It would do a figure eight, run into the entryway, then come back out to do another turn with our ankles.

"She wants you to let her in," postulated Jill.

"Hmmmm," I answered sagely, as I followed the animal into the small dark area separated from the lighted stairs beyond by a glass door. The door was locked, and as I was about to pick a bell, any bell, and get the door clicked open, I noticed that the cat's problem was not ingress but nourishment.

Someone had put out an expensive can of white chicken meat (in natural broth) but had not run the can opener completely around the track. The top had been left hinged on and somehow had gotten pushed back down. A little of the broth had seeped around the edges, but the Fifty-sixth Street cat couldn't get at the meat that so tempted and taunted her—at least not without help. I drew the trusty blade of my penknife that had seen me through so many hangnails and otherwise unopenable cartons and pried the lid back out of the cat's way. She launched herself at that chicken as if that far too expensive treat were her inalienable right. Judging from her condition, something of equal value, if not chicken, was hers on a regular basis. Chicken isn't all that nourishing for a cat, so I suspect that this was in fact treat day.

And people say cats aren't intelligent! Here was a cat with a problem, and she (the gender is a guess) figured out that she could not solve it alone. But she knew there were two-legged creatures on her planet who could solve it, who could be enlisted in her service. So she headed out and picked her marks—Jill and me—and managed to convey to us that she needed our help. The cat solved her problem by creating another problem she felt she could handle—to find someone to attend to the first problem. She did and we did and Jill and I walked on toward the theater convinced it was time to end our suffering—we had to get a cat.

Caras family cat number one was Thai Lin, a most excellent Siamese with one of the most finely honed senses of decorum I have ever encountered, in man or beast. A wild thing as a kitten, Thai Lin matured into a gorgeous seal point with a rank libido. She howled and yowled, and it began to dawn on us that we couldn't live with her unless she was spayed.

So, Thai Lin was spayed, and became ever so much more pleasant to live with after surgery. She seemed to be totally unaware of the missing parts, and I like to think she welcomed her time of peace as much as we did.

From the beginning Thai Lin homed in on Jill. She was nice enough to me—in fact, she was dearly affectionate, an ever-present lap-sitter—but she was Jill's cat and was not embarrassed in the slightest that I know it. She fussed when Jill was out and was even worse when Jill came home, scolding her as she moved at her heels from room to room. "How dare you stay away so long," was clearly what she was saying. Thai Lin's voice stopped barely short of breaking glass.

Not very long after Thai Lin took possession of Jill, we were walking down a drive near a stone wall one evening when we heard the most pitiful wailing from the woods beyond. I climbed over the wall (elected for the task because I was so agile then) and found what was left of a litter of kittens that had been tossed there in a burlap sack to die. Three of the kittens in the sack were dead and a fourth was near death. The survivor was jet-black and about as big as a minute. She bit me and then, obviously in heartfelt appreciation for my having saved her life, scratched me as I carried her to the wall and over it. I don't think she had been handled very much.

We got the waif home and Jill bottle-fed her and let her sleep in a cardboard box with a hot-water bottle piled with towels. She became Eartha Kat and turned out to be a retarded cat. She and Thai Lin had a brief period of hissing and spitting; but that passed, and Eartha assumed her role as Caras Family Critter Number Two.

Eartha was probably our least memorable cat. She was

never really affectionate, although from time to time she would try a lap for a bit. When you petted her she bumped your face with her cheek to mark you, then went her way. Being really dumb and having had a terrible start in life had marked her. Still, she was ours and we had accepted responsibility to help her lead a good life as long as that might be. It is not written, after all, that all pets must be brilliant or even charming. We often have drab brothers and sisters and, God knows, we have dull aunts and uncles. Why shouldn't an occasional pet fall short of the mark? That is no excuse to dump them. Besides, our other pets may find them enchanting. On one occasion when we were moving into a new place, we temporarily lodged our cats at my in-laws' apartment. I stopped by for lunch one day and wandered into the bedroom. My in-laws' apartment was on the seventh floor and the bedroom had a triple window arrangement. The center window was six feet wide and did not open. There were two two-foot end windows that did crank open. There was dumb Eartha in the middle of the six-foot window, outside on a very narrow ledge, obviously trying to glue herself to the glass. She had gotten out one of the side vent windows that, for some reason, was without its screen. I could not reach Eartha from either end. Had I tried, she surely would have fallen. The only thing I could do was approach the situation as quietly as possible and coax her to keep coming in the direction she was already facing. After all, she had already gotten halfway across that terrible six feet. As I walked toward the window, Eartha decided to turn around; and as I watched in horror, she vanished over the edge. She actually had more than seven floors to fall, since directly below was a cement ramp leading to the basement service entrance. I was sure Eartha was dead. Cats do land on their feet, but they can tolerate a fall from only relatively small heights.

I came out of the bedroom with a look that could not have been mistaken for anything but catastrophe. Jill and I got in the elevator and went down to collect poor Eartha's remains. But there she was down at the bottom of the ramp, eight floors below the window ledge, looking dazed and sore, but clearly alive. There was a metal canopy over a window several floors down, and she must have bounced off it and broken her fall enough to enable her to survive a plunge that would otherwise have killed her. She moaned as I carried her upstairs and placed her on a cushion. Her gums showed poor capillary return, indicating shock. We took her to a veterinarian; countless x-rays revealed no parts broken or out of place. Eartha did a lot of sleeping on soft pillows, but she got better. Now we are very careful about windows in our apartment, even though all of our cats live at our house in the country and are almost all smarter than Eartha.

Eventually Eartha got out the back door of our house and vanished. We looked for her for days, but there never was a sign of her. I would rather know a pet is dead than wonder if it is trapped and suffering. We never did know about Eartha. Poor thing, she was always so vague. I am sure her end, however it came, puzzled her. Everything else in life did.

The day came when our daughter Pamela was born, and,

as far as Thai Lin was concerned, that was it for Jill. I have never seen a cat drop someone faster. Or go for a new person more quickly. The moment that infant entered the house, she was all there was for that cat this side of Jupiter. Thai Lin was so insistent upon getting into Pamela's room that we finally had to put up a screen door with a hook and eye so we could hear our daughter and not worry about Thai Lin leaping on her. The nonsense about cats sucking the breath out of babies is just that—nonsense—but a cat will, out of curiosity or maternal instinct, jump up to where an infant is and snuggle it or wash it. The snuggling and washing are harmless enough, but landing on a sleeping child can startle it, and almost certainly isn't good for it. Still, at every opportunity, there was Thai Lin helping to change diapers, helping to bathe and feed Pamela. She could attend to nothing else. All of her other chores were neglected. In all her world, all that mattered for Thai Lin was one infant girl named Pamela.

Thai Lin's appearance had by now changed slightly. When Eartha joined us she had brought along ear mites and had passed them on to Thai Lin. Thai Lin had scratched and scratched her ears until she finally broke a blood vessel in one of them and it became as thick as a deck of playing cards. The veterinarian had to operate. The practice at the time was to sew a large button on the ear, then tape it back against the cat's head. I am not sure what the button was supposed to do, but in Thai Lin's case the cartilage was broken and the ear never moved up to its natural perky position again. She remained for the rest of her life a lop-eared cat.

No matter. It didn't bother her and it didn't bother us; and as Pamela grew into her playpen and then into a toddler, wonky-eared Thai Lin was always at hand. Pamela teethed on Thai Lin's good ear, pulled her tail, and tried to see why Thai Lin's eyes wouldn't come out; but Thai Lin didn't mind. She just purred louder. She may have been a spayed cat doomed forever to maidenhood, but in Pamela she had found her outlet. She was the Earth Mother, giver of warmth, the eternal security blanket. When Pamela began talking, she told us she had two mothers, "Mummy and Thai Lin." Thai Lin concurred. Eartha, then still around, looked vague about it all.

When Pamela went to school, Thai Lin sulked until her "child" got home, then scolded her for being away, just as she had Jill years before after her longer absences. Pamela dressed Thai Lin up, pushed her around in a doll carriage, and slept with her cat on guard every night. No matter what time we went into her room to check on our daughter, we could be sure of one thing: Thai Lin would be curled up on Pamela's bed with her front paws folded in under her creamy breast, purring with her eyes half closed. She would watch us as we adjusted the covers or pillow, watch us as we left the room and softly closed the door, and then she would have Pamela to herself for the rest of the night. It was as things were meant to be. Thai Lin purred.

In time—three years after Pamela, to be exact—our son Clay came along, and although Thai Lin thought it was dandy having two kinds of kids around the house, it was still Pamela above all others. She retained a warm spot for Jill and for me, I am sure, but nothing like the one she had for the child who now shared all secrets with her. It was a grand relationship, the kind that gives our childhoods their texture and our memories their depth.

Life has its ways of taking sharp turns, and for Pamela and Thai Lin such a turn came when Pamela was nine. We decided to spend some time living in London—good friends Stanley Kubrick and Arthur C. Clarke were going to make a film called *2001: A Space Odyssey*, and I had been invited to join the production—and Thai Lin simply couldn't go. British quarantine restrictions had become impossible, prompted by their fear of getting rabies back, now that they had eliminated it from the United Kingdom. A dog or cat had to remain in quarantine for six months, and that long in a cage didn't seem to us an act of love. So Thai Lin and Eartha, it was decided, were to live with Jill's parents, who were spending more and more time in our country house anyway. Thai Lin wouldn't be uprooted so much as she would be deprived—Pamela was being taken away from her. Pamela worried about it, lost sleep over it, and shared her mounting grief with us as the time for our departure neared.

What made it especially hard was that Pamela was mourning, not just anticipating a temporary separation. She said over and over that Thai Lin would die if she went away. She just knew it, somehow—knew that her cat would not survive without her, that in fact she wouldn't want to.

In time we settled into a small house on Hollycroft

Avenue in Hampstead Heath, just north of London. We were again petless, although a great yellow Labrador retriever named Joss who lived nearby took up with the kids and drank most of the milk they were given. Still, a pet of their own would have been nice. And Christmas was approaching.

We knew of a famed Siamese breeder outside of London named Mrs. Dunhill. Her cats were rumored to be the best ever, so we called her. She said she might be able to help us, making it very clear that that could only be if we passed muster. She was not promising to sell one of her kittens to any stranger on the phone, particularly one with a dreadful American accent.

We drove out on a miserably rainy Sunday. Mrs. Dunhill eyed us carefully and brought out a perfectly horrible five-month-old Siamese that hissed and spit and yowled at being held. No chance—even Mrs. Dunhill saw that and passed the beast off to a cattery assistant. We had tea and talked for a while, and Mrs. Dunhill admitted that the cat she had shown us was not one of her own. She was helping a friend get rid of a litter (of *Tyrannosaurus rex*? I was tempted to ask). But nine-year-old Pamela and six-year-old Clay were charming, and Mrs. Dunhill softened up over tea, after which she brought out Sumfun Abigail. Now there was a true Dunhill Siamese: beautiful, calm, gentle, a near-perfect cat. Her grandmother, Ninna, we were told, was the heroine in Keith Bryant's book *A Kitten for Christmas* and a half sister to the cat in Sir John Smythe's lovely *Beloved Cat*. Evidently only the best and brightest people knew enough to have one of Mrs. Dunhill's cats.

We made our deal, although Mrs. Dunhill was not keen on one of her best creations leaving England. We described the idyllic life her kitten would lead when eventually we returned to the Colonies, and made our way back to Hampstead, Abigail along. I was shaking from a bone-breaking brand of British flu, and with the sleet and the rain, Jill was driving as well as she could, given my moaning and Abigail's meowing. We made it alive—in my case, barely—but the important thing was that by the time we got home, cold and shivering, a remarkable creature named Abigail had somehow become a part of our lives.

We anticipated terrible problems back home if this new Siamese cat were to become especially attached to Pamela. But as it turned out, while both Pamela and Clay enjoyed their Christmas present enormously, Pamela understood, and never allowed herself to become the focus of Abigail's attention. Abigail slept on our bed, not Pamela's, an arrangement we made sure of by the judicious use of open and closed doors. We were determined to head off trouble before it arose. Pamela had stopped mourning Thai Lin's anticipated death, but she was still worried about her, and the flow of letters from home failed to reassure her. It was always in the back of her mind that she had abandoned her closest friend.

The situation was probably helped by the addition to our household of an exceedingly strange trio of pets. We were making *2001* at the MGM studios in Borehamwood in Hertfordshire. One of the crew had been on location with another film in Africa earlier in the year and had come home with three bush babies—small, nocturnal primates that have bushy tails and weigh about as much as a postage stamp. This film person had all three bush babies in a terrible little cage, and they were not well. Their tails had gone all bare. I bought them from him out of pity, and that is how Patrick, Broderick, and Fredrick, "the Ick brothers," joined our menagerie.

Bush babies can be fiercely threatening little devils, and they bounce around like rubber balls. Abigail (we had dropped "Sumfun" as being a bit too cutesy) loved the bush babies. They threatened her by going up on their hind legs and spreading their arms wide while hissing like komodo lizards. Abigail thought that was just swell. She could spend hours getting the bouncing bush babies to do their threat displays. The spectacle never ceased to amaze her—or us, for that matter.

Spring came, the bush babies had furry tails again, and Abigail had grown into a great beauty. Fortunately, she was still clearly Jill's cat. The time was nearing for our return to the states, and Pamela and Clay began packing their many London-acquired possessions. The plan was for Jill, the kids, and the animals to sail home on the *France*, and I would follow a month later by plane. Three days before they were to sail, the cable arrived. Thai Lin had died. It was a terrible moment for Pamela, however convinced she had been of its coming—and then the most extraordinary thing happened. That very night, instead of coming to our room as she always had, Abigail went to Pamela's room, jumped up on her bed and snuggled up. And, just as Thai Lin had done, she abandoned Jill. She became, on the day we learned of Thai Lin's death, Pamela's cat.

Anyone who has owned cats and dogs has had such things happen, or knows of them happening to other people; but who can explain them? How did that cat know? What, if any, message was sent by the tone of Pamela's voice, or Jill's, or mine? Was it body posture or was it something else?

Thai Lin lay dead a hemisphere away when Abigail somehow knew there was no longer any problem with rivalry and gave herself for the rest of her life to lonely, needy, catless Pamela. Who can say how these things work?

Polite Company

Peter Gethers

Recently, I was in Paris with my rather astonishing and extremely handsome Scottish Fold cat, Norton. We were having dinner with Danielle, an old friend of mine who lives in the Seventeenth arrondissement, and her daughter, Priscilla. I met Priscilla when she was four years old and the only English sentence she knew was, "I like ze Beeg Mac 'amburgair." By the night of our dinner, Priscilla was no longer four. She was twenty-three, spoke fluent English, and wanted to take us to a restaurant where her boyfriend worked. Which means I'm getting longer in the tooth (not to mention thicker around the middle).

I say "we" and "us," by the way, because no one was all that excited just to see *me*. Norton was the star attraction. Danielle had made it quite clear that they would certainly be happy if I came along, but they were *really* interested in my little gray pal as their primary dinner companion. Danielle even let me know that the owner of the restaurant, when told about Norton and his adventures traveling the globe, had insisted that *le chat* come to dinner as her very special guest.

When we arrived at the restaurant, Bistro d'Albert, a

charming and perfect place that could exist only in France, Norton was greeted the way I imagine Ike was when he arrived at the Champs Élysées immediately following D-day. He was given, as he always is, his own chair, which he settled into quite comfortably. The owner, a typical somewhere-over-forty-year-old blond Frenchwoman for whom you'd happily give up the rest of your life if she'd only so much as smile at you, smiled up a storm. But not at me. Oh, no. At my innocent-looking furry friend, who, just to annoy me, I'm sure, purred like a motorboat, rolled over on his back, and practically begged the owner and all of her gorgeous waitresses to come over and scratch his stomach, which, of course, they did. Meanwhile, I was doing my best to order, but I couldn't get anyone to even look at me.

Eventually, the waitresses returned to their regular duties, went about their work, and dinner settled into a normal routine. The three humans had the specialty of the house, and the cat worked away on some broiled chicken and a small bowl of milk.

One of the most satisfying things about being in Europe is that animals are treated with enormous respect. You can go into the very best, most expensive restaurants in Paris and it is almost guaranteed that someone will have brought his or her dog along for the meal. No one bats an eye, no one thinks it odd. The general feeling is that a dog has as much right to eat at Robuchon as any human. This night, at Bistro d'Albert, *five* people brought their dogs along. Which meant that at some point—I think it was during the cheese course—Norton looked up from his *lait froid*

20

to find five curious canines of varying sizes and tempera-
ments sitting in a circle around his chair. One of them
growled. Another worked up his courage, stuck his nose
right in Norton's face, and took a particularly antagonistic
sniff. The dogs seemed to be of the opinion that Parisian
restaurants were *their* domain and that cats should stay
where they belonged—curled up by the fireplace in a turn-
of-the-century apartment or prowling around a garden
searching for tasty mice. Certainly they did *not* belong in
places where they could actually compete for affection,
much less the *boeuf bourguignon*. For just a moment, the
room froze. I didn't know if French people had ever heard of
The Gunfight at the O.K. Corral—but I had a feeling they
were about to. Except that Norton, in the peacekeeping role
of Wyatt Earp, simply looked determinedly at his ring of
potential tormentors, stared each of them, one by one,
straight in the eye, then calmly went back to eating his
chicken and sipping his milk. When one dog barked,
demanding a little more attention, Norton finished chewing
his last piece of chicken, then glanced at the barker with
pity, as if to say, "Please. This is France. You're embarrassing
me. Haven't you read your Sartre?"

That was the end of the confrontation. Deflated, the
dogs went back to their respective masters and sat under their
own tables, hoping to receive a morsel of food now that their
bluff had been called.

The rest of the dinner went fairly smoothly until it
came time for dessert. Danielle, Priscilla, and I ordered our

mousse and our pastries, and when we were served, the chef emerged from the kitchen with a big bowl of ice cream. Priscilla had mentioned to him that Norton was an ice-cream fiend.

"Zees is for ze incredible cat," he told me. "I made *chocolat*—his favoreet."

Now, Norton likes his chocolate ice cream, no question about it. But he's also quite particular. He loves Ben & Jerry's. Häagen-Dazs gets an A-plus. He will eat frozen yogurt and ice milk but only in an emergency. If offered some chocolate *non*-fat frozen yogurt, he will turn his back disgustedly after one lick, making you feel as if you'd just offered a Sabrettes chili dog to the Queen of England.

The chef dug a spoon into his ice cream and held it up toward Norton. The cat eagerly took a lick, hesitated, gave some thought to what he'd just eaten—and disdainfully turned his back on the chef. I immediately had visions of the chef pulling out a glove, slapping me, and challenging me to a duel—and I was not so far off.

"It's not posseeble," he told me, totally bewildered. "Our ice cream is superb!"

"I'm sure it is," I agreed. "He's probably just full."

"But Priscilla told me he loves ze ice cream."

"Why don't you try giving him another taste," I suggested, although I knew my cat well enough to know this would be a useless gesture. By this time, the owner had come to the table to see what the problem was. When I explained, I could see the existential pain in her eyes.

"We have never 'ad a complaint in all our years," she told me. "Zis is outrageous."

"Give him another taste," a waitress urged.

So the chef held out a second spoonful of the stuff. Norton licked cautiously, looked at the brown lump, and, if cats can shake their heads—and I am one hundred percent certain that mine can—he shook his head. *No way*, is basically what he was saying.

Thus ended the meal. The chef stalked back into the kitchen, offended and insulted. The owner made it chillingly clear that the cat was not nearly as special as she had been led to believe. And I was fairly certain that the next time the Larousse French/English Dictionary put in the phrase "ugly American," my photo would be next to the definition.

I gathered Norton in my arms, tried to figure out how I could explain to a cat about the concepts of tact and eating to be polite, gave up, and stuck him back in his cloth shoulder bag, his favorite mode of transportation.

As we were going out the door, one of the waitresses pulled me aside.

"Your leetle cat," she said. "'E was right."

I looked at her curiously and she explained.

"Ze chef, he made a batch of ice cream and eet was not good," she went on. "He thought he could put one over on ze cat and get rid of it." She put her hand on the top of Norton's head and scratched him, something that ranks in his top three activities. "Zat is a very impressive cat," she said. "And his taste is soo-pairb."

"I never doubted it," I told her and looked at my "leetle cat," just a bit awed. He looked back at me, dubious. "Honest," I said to him, and held my hand over my heart. "I never doubted you for a minute."

My Cat, Cyrus

Clea Simon

As I type this, Cyrus is walking across my computer. While I was opening up this file, he jumped to the sofa beside me and then stepped neatly by my hands and onto my laptop. Carefully placing one velvet paw before the other, he has walked above the keys and across the space bar to take up a seat beside me and then pawed delicately at the book lying by my side. Seeing what he was up to, I removed the book to the table and pushed the laptop a bit farther away from my body. He muttered what I interpret as satisfaction at my making room for him, a soft "mr-r-ah"—half aspiration, half mew—as he turned and kneaded the part of my hip left exposed by the laptop, before settling down beside me to purr and, probably, to sleep as I work.

Cyrus has developed a new set of personality traits as he has aged; and I find myself adjusting to him, to his emerging elder-statesman personality, much as I did to the rambunctious kitten that I adopted out of my friend Kathei's litter more than sixteen years before. These days we toss around the catnip toys a lot less. A few nights ago I did let the belt of my terry-cloth robe dangle, afraid to hope, and was thrilled when he stalked and pounced on it, as in the old days—that dragging bit of cloth becoming once more the most elusive of prey. But such moments of play are fewer now; and more often I find myself sitting beside my old friend, sometimes stroking him as he stares into space and sometimes watching him sleep. He seems to desire my presence more these days, even if it's just to remain at the breakfast table a few minutes longer while he surveys the yard from the kitchen window, to share attack strategies for the squirrels that brazenly stare back from the lawn, and to size up birds made more visible by the falling leaves. I tarry longer now, waiting for him to tire of his watch and find a comfortable place to curl up and nap, or for him to remove himself from my presence of his own will for reasons that I cannot begin to guess. I want to just be with him more now, as he too experiences autumn.

We make a quiet couple these days, and that is a comfort to me. Some of this, I know, is fear of loss, fear of the inevitable that I can't avoid each time I pick up his diminished bulk or feel the bones of his spine and pelvis as I stroke his gently vibrating back. Some, though, comes from him, from his seemingly increased desire to be with me, to find me in the room nearby when he wakes up. Often I am; I want him to be happy, and he usually seems to know that I will be there or will be only a room or a hallway away. He wasn't always so confident, and these days when he wakes and seeks me out, at work or sitting with a book, I remember such a time. Once, when a kitten, during a visit to my parent's house, he woke up in my old bedroom alone and believed himself lost, abandoned as he slept. I had gone downstairs and left him sleeping there, a perfect silver circle of fur arranged neatly on the coverlet. I'm ashamed to say I thought little about him as I chatted on the phone downstairs, calling old acquaintances and making plans—until I heard the plaintive cry, the "ow!" of a lost, lonely kitten. "OW!" was ringing ridiculously loudly from up the stairs. "OW!"

"Cyrus, what's wrong?" I remember responding, putting down the receiver to run to the foot of the stairs. "Cyrus!"

And standing at the top of the tall staircase, eyes blinking still from sleep, was my kitten. He was calm again, looking down at me, having been drawn most likely by the sound of my voice and comforted by the sight of me, by the assurance of my presence. "Mr-up-up-up," he chattered as he made his way down the steep stairs, each step taller than his round baby body was long. His voice had become chatty, almost conversational. And as much as I can know anything about a cat, I am convinced he had wakened alone in a strange place and panicked. My voice and then the sight of me calmed him immediately, and he hopped his way downstairs to continue exploring this new territory, confident in the security of my continued presence.

Cyrus has always been a people cat. Early on, I attributed his desire for my company to his first experiences with my kind and his own. My kitten, who grew up so handsome, was the runt of his litter, less energetic than his peppy siblings, smaller and less healthy, and I chose him for all the wrong reasons. When Kathei's momma cat had her litter and my friend invited me over, I probably should have opted for one of the livelier babies, one of the other gray or black or orange furballs that ran toward me or fled, chasing a noisy toy, or that ignored me entirely to nurse lustily. But my heart was taken by the one who remained when Kathei and I and her daughter loomed over the cluster of kittens. For as some scattered onto the rug and one or two others dug into their momma's belly seeking a nipple, one tiny gray kitten just sat and looked up at me. I felt chosen.

Afterward, I told myself that this kitten might end up ignored by its mother or bullied by its bigger, stronger peers, and that was reason enough for my solicitous care. Sure enough, when I brought my new pet home a few weeks later, my roommate's irascible adult cat, Chenille, responded thus. Not that Chenille, a rather neurotic and overweight calico, whose name I have changed to protect those who undoubtedly loved her, beat up on Cyrus. Rather she seemed resentful, even paranoid; and if I seem to be somewhat the same in my description of her, I rest easy believing that other new mothers would judge a similar bully the same way. For what Chenille did was cruel, but also rather odd, and convinced me that she was not an emotionally healthy cat.

Chenille, with all of a big three-bedroom apartment to choose from, seemed to decide that she couldn't share her litter box with Cyrus. Not her food, perhaps because I soon realized that I needed to provide private dishes. Not her bed—Cyrus shared mine—but her litter box. Now, I have since learned that such territoriality might not be unusual, but I still believe that older cat's mode of enforcement was.

To protect her turf, quite literally, Chenille would sit in the litter box for hours. She would just squat there, waiting, and hiss at my little fellow whenever he tried to approach. *This is my box, the last bastion of my privacy,* that fat, ornery cat hissed. *Go away.*

I should have realized that there was more going on there than just feline politics. At twenty-three, I also should, perhaps, have been wiser in the ways of people, and of roommates. Because by the time I had gotten my kitten—without, I will admit, getting more than grudging, conditional acceptance from my then-roommates—I had already begun to have my own problems with our shared living quarters.

First there was the problem of the sewing room, as the large apartment's dining room had come to be known. With a big table in the kitchen, and—to be honest—with many of our meals eaten in front of the television in the living room, this sunny room lit by its big windows and door onto our porch had come to be used as a workroom. When I moved in, the newcomer joining a long-settled unit of two, I had observed the central table strewn with papers and cloth, seen the sideboard piled high with books and catalogs, and figured that it was a common workspace—a catchall back-of-the-building room outside our bedrooms and separate from the tidy living room, which guests could see as soon as they came through our front door.

Since I wrote rather than sewed in my spare time, I figured I could stake out a corner of the room for my own work, specifically for my computer and printer. That was my hobby, I figured; though in my heart I was always hoping that the words I churned out would take me away from the chemical smells and triplicate reports of pithed cats. (I briefly worked as a secretary in a physiology lab. Don't ask.) Therefore, one afternoon when I'd gotten home, I set about moving my equipment from my tiny, crowded bedroom into that sunny space. First I carried in the dowdy blue Kaypro that I wrote my essays and reviews on—a heavy boxlike computer that would have dwarfed today's machines (except for its minuscule, recessed screen) but which, even with its gray metal stand, took up less space than their Singers and notion boxes, not to mention the dressmaker's dummies that stood nearby. Then I carried in my carton of printer paper, which sat neatly below the printer, and threaded the first page through the old-style dot matrix printer's jaws, ready to go. When I stepped back into the doorway, my entire setup nearly disappeared in the colorful mess made by bolts of cloth, by pattern books and by patterns. *Good*, I thought, *I'm fitting in.* I was ready to work; however, this was not to be.

"What is all this machinery doing here?" I remember hearing from my room as I changed from my secretarial skirt and hose. "What are all these papers?"

"That's my computer," I tried to explain. "I thought I'd move my work stuff into the workroom."

"But it's the sewing room!"

"Yeah, but I don't sew."

"It's for sewing!" We might have gone back and forth longer, but I doubt it. At twenty-three, I lacked the confidence to argue further. My move into the supposed common space had been rejected, and the computer and its paraphernalia moved back into the one room to which my share of the rent inarguably gave me rights.

Then there was the question of curfew. Not that we had one, not that we'd ever discussed one. And at that age, I had the energy, the desire, and the camaraderie to go out fairly often, and certainly on the weekends. To top it off, I was finally getting assignments from the local paper to write about some of the bands I saw and heard, musicians whom I met and drank with until closing time. My roommates at the time were less social. One had a steady boyfriend, but they usually stayed in. And the other, well, she would sometimes go out after work and would sometimes try blind dates. But every time the phone rang and it wasn't for her, her resentment was made obvious by her terse, often inaccurate messages. And every time I went out buffed and polished and woke up glowing from whatever adventures the night had brought my way, my good mood added fuel to her simmering jealousy.

Further problems arose when she began to focus on my (to me very reasonable) behavior of sleeping late on Saturday mornings, catching up on my rest after a full week of work and, usually, nights of play. Even though we were all in our twenties, all healthy, and more or less single, such a life, clearly, was not acceptable to my unattached flatmate, who not only began to get up earlier and earlier to start her Saturday cleaning, but began ramming the vacuum cleaner hard against my door as soon as the cleaning commenced. I got the message, and although I didn't stop staying out late with my friends, I did begin wearing earplugs to bed.

No wonder, then, that their shared cat acted as she did. Chenille, fat and irritable, was simply following her owners' cues when she hissed at my kitten or cuffed him as he bent toward the food dishes in the kitchen corner. But when Chenille began spending increasing amounts of time performing her most perverse habit, that of hoarding the litter box, my Cyrus, the runt of his litter and certainly the smallest and newest inhabitant of our apartment, took action.

"Clea!" I heard the bellow even through the earplugs early the next morning. "Get in here right now!" My roommate's voice was coming from the bathroom and so I stumbled from my slumbers into the small room at the end of the hall. I have never seen a woman more red in the face. She stared at me. I tried to focus. She gestured downward, into the sink, her hand still holding the toothbrush she had obviously just picked up. There, in the basin, was a neat pile of poop. Cyrus was nowhere to be found.

In retrospect, I wonder that we both accepted that my cat had made the mess. After all, even when one cat is still growing and the other mature, once first kittenhood is past, their poop does not look that different. Clearly, my roommate had assumed the worst because I was the unruly newcomer, as she would put it, and therefore my pet must be the more bestial of the two. And I? Well, I had seen how the bigger, older cat had tried to bully my kitten, and if I didn't yet have the self-possession to champion myself, I instinctively bristled to defend my pet. Plus, in my heart of hearts, I admired the solution that I believed Cyrus's innate intelligence had found: He had, after all, defecated in a basin, in a contained space, as near to the litter box as he was allowed to get. The fact that he made a statement about our presence in the apartment was another thing altogether, and I am not entirely certain that it was not a conscious gesture on my tiny feline friend's part.

However, in this situation I too was the runt, or at least the one with the least power. And though I tried not to share the wisdom and humor I saw in his actions, as I cleaned up, I was already laughing. Nothing would beat the look on that woman's face, I told myself, and that was worth all. Cyrus and I moved out a month or two later, but if there had been any doubt about our relationship before, our bond was cemented from that morning on.

I should pause here to discuss Chenille, since she too was a cat and she too was bonded with a woman, primarily with the happier of my two roommates. She was, in my biased view, an extremely neurotic cat, overweight to the point of unhealthiness and unfriendly to anyone who was not her one person. But perhaps she had reason. Perhaps she came from a bad home, and perhaps my roommate was the one person who cared—the sympathetic soul who rescued her and gave her love and clearly fed her all she wanted. I look back on her and see an ordinary tabby, her subtle tiger stripes dimmed in my memory by her offensive behavior. But the beauty, and the bond, was not, in this case, for me.

After all, when Cyrus first came into my life, he wasn't yet the furry sweetheart he would become. He was a small kitten with a big spirit, and he staked a lion-size claim on my heart; but he was more than a bit awkward. Even when we moved into our next place, with the much more amiable Susan, he had his share of mishaps: I can still hear his howling as the cloth front of my stereo speaker became dislodged during his ascent up the tall cabinet's front. Despite my quick run down the hall, I didn't get there in time to catch it, or dislodge his panicked claws; and he was still clinging as the cloth-covered frame fell over, bearing his small frame with it. And I remember the time that either Susan or I had forgotten to replace the fireplace screen, and Cyrus decided to explore that previously forbidden space. We returned home to find perfect, rounded soot prints all over the rug, around the bathtub, and along the kitchen counters, where he would never dare venture in my presence.

Until he filled out under my care, he went through a period of looking a tad ratty too, his mite-bitten ears scratched into scabs and his green eyes runny and sad. The cat he grew into couldn't have been less a misfit, or more handsome. "What is his breeding?" I've often been asked. "Is he a show cat?" After perusing countless cat books and matching his smoky, slightly tiger-striped back, wide gray and white ruff, and elegantly plumed tail to one such specialty breed, I'm often tempted to respond that, yes, he is a show cat—a Norwegian forest cat, bred for his fine coat and green eyes, the intelligent point of his face and large tufted ears. But the truth is, of course, that he's a mix, just like ninety percent of the pet cats in this country.

And while others admire a magnificent beast with a proud ruff, with a flag of a tail that arches up in an elegant sweep of long, silky hair, they do not always see the cat I do. They never notice, for example, how his leonine profile veers from the classic into a slightly bumpy nose. They don't see that my perfect show cat has a Roman nose, rather like mine—a Brando nose that, had I not known better, would have hinted to me of a misspent youth and boxing rings. And as much as I admire Cyrus's lush coat, his stunning tail and ears, over the years it is that nose I have come to love most of all, savoring the times he would let me stroke its dark smoked velvet. Yes, he's a handsome cat, marvelously so, but I would love him no less were he still bat-faced and scrawny. He's my cat, and that's what makes him special.

All Mine

Marion Bond West

Marion, why don't you get another cat?" a friend suggested one day last spring. "You loved Minnie."

"That's exactly why I don't want another one now," I said. "That cat broke my heart. I'm not ready to go through something like that again."

Two years had passed since we put Minnie down, at age seventeen. I still missed her every day. I missed her spying out our living room curtains at the bird feeder, running to rub against my legs every time she heard the false promise of the electric can opener. There were those luminous yellow eyes blinking "hello" to Gene and me when we walked in the door, and the little thump she made when she jumped up on our bed at night and settled down contentedly between us. I missed that thump. But most of all, there were those recurring dreams I had.

"Besides," I told my friend, "things are easier now. No more cat hair all over everything. And Gene and I can take last-minute trips without feeling guilty." No, it wouldn't make any sense to get another cat. End of story.

Not quite. That night I had the dream again—cats of all kinds trailing me as if I were the pied piper of tuna. *Stop it,*

Marion! I told myself in the morning. *Dream cats aren't real cats. They never die and leave you grieving.*

I sat down with the newspaper at breakfast. An announcement jumped out at me. "Pet Adoption Day at the Oconee Library. Saturday, ten A.M. Give an Abandoned Pet a Home."

Abandoned. That's got to be one of the saddest words in the English language. I said a quick prayer. "Please, may all those poor, lonely, frightened animals find a home." To myself, I added, *But not with me. Not until I'm ready. Not until this pain stops.*

Saturday morning I set out to do my usual errands. First stop, the supermarket. Or so I thought. Inexplicably, I found myself taking the turnoff to the library instead. *I'm just going to see if any new books have arrived.*

The Oconee County Animal Control van was parked opportunistically near the sidewalk leading to the library entrance. I marched past the dogs in their cages, my eyes focused straight ahead. *Don't even look.*

I nearly fell over a table set up by the library door. A woman sat there smiling. Beside her was a small animal carrier.

"Can I help you?" she asked.

"No, thanks," I said. *Keep walking, Marion. This is dangerous.*

"Meow!" The sound emanated from the carrier. I stopped in my tracks. "Looking for a new friend?" the woman asked.

"Not me. Not after my last cat died." There, I'd said it.

Now it was safe for me to peek through the door of the pet carrier. One look and I'd be on my way.

A pair of large amber eyes like polished marbles gazed back at me. *What took you so long?* they seemed to say, and for a crazy moment, I thought the cat had been expecting me. *Marion! No more cats.* But she was so petite and delicate, long-haired, black-and-white. "Hi, girl," I whispered. I touched her nose through the wire door. She began to purr as though a tiny switch had been turned on.

"How long has she been at the shelter?" I asked.

"She was dropped off a few weeks ago with three newborn kittens," the woman said. "The kittens died. We had a hard time taking them from her. She was a good little mama cat."

"Oh, girl," I said, "don't you worry, somebody nice will come and adopt you." The cat pressed her head against my hand, and I couldn't resist asking, "Can I take her out of the carrier?"

"Sorry," the woman said. "Only if you're thinking of taking her."

I wasn't.

I sat on the sidewalk and watched the cat wash her fur. *Lord, this pretty little cat deserves a good home. Please find someone who is ready to love her.*

People stopped by to see the dogs and fill out adoption forms. I was content just to sit with the little black-and-white cat. If I could purr, I might have. I checked my watch. I'd been sitting there almost an hour! "We're not that busy right now,"

the woman from the shelter said. "Suppose I let you hold her."
She unlatched the carrier door.

"Come here, girl," I said. The cat reached out and put a
tiny white paw on my hand. She paused, looked up, and
meowed. Cats can be aloof. This one acted very familiar. I
lifted her out, and she nestled against my neck, all fuzzy and
warm. *Purrrrrr.*

"What would you name her?" the woman asked.

It just popped out of my mouth. "Girl Friend." Where on
earth had that come from? "But there's no way I can take her,"
I said quickly. "I'm not ready."

"Too bad. She's really taken to you."

Girl Friend rubbed her cheek against mine. I didn't want
to fall in love. That's the thing about love, though: you can't
decide on it, and I couldn't deny it. I was officially in love,
ready or not. *Okay, Lord, I know I asked you to find this cat a
home. But this isn't what I had in mind.*

I put the cat back in the carrier and filled out an adoption form. The woman told me it would take a few days to be
approved. "Sit tight, Girl Friend," I said. "I'll be back for you."

"I've found us a new cat," I told Gene when I got home.
He gave me a sidelong glance, but he didn't say anything. For
the next three days all I thought about was that cat, her nose
pressing into my hand, her purr that vibrated through my
whole arm when I petted her. Finally the woman from the
shelter called. "Your adoption application went through. She's
all yours."

In no time Girl Friend was exploring our house, making

herself at home. She investigated under the beds, among the closet shelves, inside the grand piano. Then she ran to the sink and meowed until I turned on the faucet for her to drink.

I went to bed that first night fairly confident that I wouldn't dream of cats. I was just drifting off when I felt a familiar little thump on the bed. Girl Friend padded up the covers and snuggled down between us. *Purrrrrr.* Her amber eyes blinked. And to think I had almost missed out on this! All along I had said I wasn't ready. For two years I grieved for Minnie. Sometimes we can get lost in our own pain. But there's always a way out, even if we don't see it. I'd asked the Lord to give Girl Friend what she needed. He gave me exactly what I needed too.

Olly and Ginny
Settle In

James Herriot

As a cat lover, it irked me that my own cats couldn't stand the sight of me. Ginny and Olly were part of the family now. We were devoted to them; and whenever we had a day out, the first thing Helen did on our return was to open the back door and feed them. The cats knew this very well and were either sitting on the flat top of the wall, waiting for her, or ready to trot down from the log shed which was their home.

We had been to Brawton on our half-day and they were there as usual as Helen put out a dish of food and a bowl of milk for them on the wall.

"Olly, Ginny," she murmured as she stroked the furry coats. The days had long gone when they refused to let her touch them. Now they rubbed against her hand in delight, arching and purring and, when they were eating, she ran her hand repeatedly along their backs. They were such gentle little animals, their wildness expressed only in fear; and now, with her, that fear had gone. My children and some from the village had won their confidence too and were allowed to give them a careful caress, but they drew the line at Herriot.

Like now, for instance, when I quietly followed Helen

out and moved towards the wall. Immediately they left the food and retreated to a safe distance where they stood, still arching their backs but, as ever, out of reach. They regarded me without hostility, but as I held out a hand they moved further away.

"Look at the little beggars!" I said. "They still won't have anything to do with me."

It was frustrating since, throughout my years in veterinary practice, cats had always intrigued me; and I had found that this helped me in my dealings with them. I felt I could handle them more easily than most people because I liked them and they sensed it. I rather prided myself on my cat technique, a sort of feline bedside manner, and was in no doubt that I had an empathy with the entire species and that they all liked me. In fact, if the truth were told, I fancied myself as a cats' pinup. Not so, ironically, with these two—the ones to whom I had become so deeply attached.

It was a bit hard, I thought, because I had doctored them and probably saved their lives when they had cat flu. Did they remember that, I wondered? If they did it still didn't give me the right, apparently, to lay a finger on them. And, indeed, what they certainly did seem to remember was that it was I who had netted them and then shoved them into a cage before I neutered them. I had the feeling that whenever they saw me, it was that net and cage which was uppermost in their minds.

I could only hope that time would bring an understanding between us but; as it turned out, fate was to conspire against me for a long time still. Above all, there was the business of Olly's coat. Unlike his sister, he was a long-haired cat and as such was subject to constant tangling and knotting of his fur. If he had been an ordinary domesticated feline, I would have combed him out as soon as trouble arose; but since I couldn't even get near him, I was helpless. We had had him about two years when Helen called me to the kitchen.

"Just look at him!" she said. "He's a dreadful sight!"

I peered through the window. Olly was indeed a bit of a scarecrow, with his matted fur and dangling knots in cruel contrast with his sleek and beautiful little sister.

"I know, I know. But what can I do?" I was about to turn away when I noticed something. "Wait a minute, there's a couple of horrible, big lumps hanging below his neck. Take these scissors and have a go at them—a couple of quick snips and they'll be off."

Helen gave me an anguished look. "Oh, we've tried this before. I'm not a vet, and anyway, he won't let me do that. He'll let me pet him, but this is something else."

"I know that, but have a go. There's nothing to it, really." I pushed a pair of curved scissors into her hand and began to call instructions through the window. "Right now, get your fingers behind that big dangling mass. Fine, fine! Now up with your scissors and—"

But at the first gleam of steel, Olly was off and away up the hill. Helen turned to me in despair. "It's no good, Jim, it's hopeless—he won't let me cut even one lump off and he's covered with them."

I looked at the dishevelled little creature standing at a safe distance from us. "Yes, you're right. I'll have to think of something."

Thinking of something entailed doping Olly so that I could get at him, and my faithful Nembutal capsules sprang immediately to mind. This oral anaesthetic had been a valued ally on countless occasions where I had to deal with unapproachable animals, but this was different. With the other cases, my patients had been behind closed doors, but Olly was outside with all the wide countryside to roam in. I couldn't have him going to sleep somewhere out there where a fox or other predator might get him. I would have to watch him all the time.

It was a time for decisions, and I drew myself up. "I'll have a go at him this Sunday," I told Helen. "It's usually a bit quieter, and I'll ask Siegfried to stand in for me in an emergency."

When the day arrived, Helen went out and placed two meals of chopped fish on the wall, one of them spiked with the contents of my Nembutal capsule. I crouched behind the window, watching intently as she directed Olly to the correct portion, and holding my breath as he sniffed at it suspiciously. His hunger soon overcame his caution, and he licked the bowl clean with evident relish.

Now we started the tricky part. If he decided to explore the fields, as he often did, I would have to be right behind him. I stole out of the house as he sauntered back up the slope to the open log shed, and to my vast relief he settled down in his own particular indentation in the straw and began to wash himself.

As I peered through the bushes, I was gratified to see that very soon he was having difficulty with his face—licking his hind paw, then toppling over as he brought it up to his cheek.

I chuckled to myself. This was great. Another few minutes and I'd have him.

And so it turned out. Olly seemed to conclude that he was tired of falling over and it wouldn't be a bad idea to have a nap. After gazing drunkenly around him, he curled up in the straw.

I waited a short time, then, with all the stealth of an Indian brave on the trail, I crept from my hiding place and tiptoed to the shed. Olly wasn't flat out—I hadn't dared give him the full anaesthetic dose in case I had been unable to track him—but he was deeply sedated. I could pretty well do what I wanted with him.

As I knelt down and began to snip away with my scissors, he opened his eyes and made a feeble attempt to struggle, but it was no good and I worked my way quickly through the ravelled fur. I wasn't able to make a particularly tidy job because he was wriggling slightly all the time, but I clipped off all the huge unsightly knots which used to get caught in the bushes, and which must have been horribly uncomfortable, and soon I had a growing heap of black hair by my side.

I noticed that Olly wasn't only moving; he was watching me. Dazed as he was, he knew me, all right, and his eyes told me all. *It's you again!* he was saying. *I might have known!*

When I had finished, I lifted him into a cat cage and placed it on the straw. "Sorry, old lad," I said, "but I can't let you go free till you've wakened up completely."

Olly gave me a sleepy stare, but his sense of outrage was evident. *So you've dumped me in here again. You don't change much, do you?*

By teatime he was fully recovered and I was able to release him. He looked so much better without the ugly tangles, but he didn't seem impressed; and as I opened the cage he gave me a single disgusted look and sped away.

Helen was enchanted with my handiwork and she pointed eagerly at the two cats on the wall the next morning. "Doesn't he look smart! Oh, I'm so glad you managed to do him; it was really worrying me. And he must feel so much better."

I felt a certain smug satisfaction as I looked through the window. Olly indeed was almost unrecognisable as the scruffy animal of yesterday, and there was no doubt I had dramatically altered his life and relieved him of a constant discomfort. But my burgeoning bubble of self-esteem was pricked the instant I put my head round the back door. He had just started to enjoy his breakfast, but at the sight of me he streaked away faster than ever before and disappeared far over the hilltop. I turned sadly back into the kitchen. Olly's opinion of me had dropped several more notches. Wearily I poured a cup of tea. It was a hard life.

Months passed without any thawing of relations between me and our two wild cats, and I noticed with growing apprehension that Olly's long coat was reverting to its previous disreputable state. The familiar knots and tangles were reappearing, and within a year it was as bad as ever. It became more obvious every day that I had to do something about it. But could I trick him again? I had to try.

I made the same preparations, with Helen placing the Nembutal-laden food on the wall, but this time Olly sniffed, licked, then walked away. We tried at his next mealtime, but he examined the food with deep suspicion and turned away from it. It was very clear that he sensed there was something afoot.

Hovering in my usual position at the kitchen window, I turned to Helen. "I'm going to have to try to catch him."

"Catch him? With your net, do you mean?"

"No, no. That was all right when he was a kitten. I'd never get near him now."

"How, then?"

I looked out at the scruffy black creature on the wall. "Well, maybe I can hide behind you when you feed him and grab him and bung him into the cage. I could take him down to the surgery then, give him a general anaesthetic, and make a proper job of him."

"Grab him? And then fasten him in the cage?" Helen said incredulously. "It sounds impossible to me."

"Yes, I know, but I've grabbed a few cats in my time and I can move fast. If only I can keep hidden. We'll try tomorrow."

My wife looked at me, wide-eyed. I could see that she had little faith.

Next morning she placed some delicious, fresh-chopped raw haddock on the wall. It was the cats' favourite. They were not particularly partial to cooked fish, but this was irresistible.

The open cage lay hidden from sight. The cats stalked along the wall, Ginny sleek and shining, Olly a pathetic sight with his ravelled hair and ugly knotted appendages dangling from his neck and body. Helen made her usual fuss of the two of them, then, as they descended happily on the food, she returned to the kitchen where I was lurking.

"Right, now," I said. "I want you to walk out very slowly again and I am going to be tucked in behind you. When you go up to Olly, he'll be concentrating on the fish and maybe won't notice me."

Helen made no reply as I pressed myself into her back, in close contact from head to toe.

"Okay, off we go." I nudged her left leg with mine and we shuffled off through the door, moving as one.

"This is ridiculous," Helen wailed. "It's like a music hall act."

Nuzzling the back of her neck, I hissed into her ear, "Quiet, just keep going."

As we advanced on the wall, double-bodied, Helen reached out and stroked Olly's head, but he was too busy with the haddock to look up. He was there, chest-high, within a couple of feet of me. I'd never have a better chance. Shooting my hand round Helen, I seized him by the scruff of his neck; held him, a flurry of flailing black limbs, for a couple of seconds; then pushed him into the cage. As I crashed the lid down, a desperate paw appeared at one end; but I thrust it back and slotted home the steel rod. There was no escape now.

I lifted the cage onto the wall with Olly and me at eye level, and I flinched as I met his accusing stare through the bars. *Oh no, not again! I don't believe this!* it said. *Is there no end to your treachery?*

In truth, I felt pretty bad. The poor cat, terrified as he was by my assault, had not tried to scratch or bite. It was like the other occasions—his only thought was to get away. I couldn't blame him for thinking the worst of me.

However, I told myself, the end result was going to be a fine, handsome animal again. "You won't know yourself, old chap," I said to the petrified little creature, crouched in his cage on the car seat by my side as we drove to the surgery. "I'm going to fix you up properly, this time. You're going to look great and feel great."

Siegfried had offered to help me; and when we got the cat on the table, a trembling Olly submitted to being handled and to the intravenous anaesthetic. As he lay sleeping peacefully, I started on the awful tangled fur with a fierce pleasure, snipping and trimming and then going over him with the electric clippers, followed by a long combing until the last tiny knot was removed. I had only given him a makeshift hairdo before, but this was the full treatment.

Siegfried laughed when I held him up after I had finished. "Looks ready to win any cat show." he said.

I thought of his words the next morning when the cats came to the wall for their breakfast. Ginny was always beautiful; but she was almost outshone by her brother, as he strutted along, his smooth, lustrous fur gleaming in the sunshine.

Helen was enchanted at his appearance and kept running her hand along his back as though she couldn't believe the transformation. I, of course, was in my usual position, peeking furtively from the kitchen window. It was going to be a long time before I even dared to show myself to Olly.

It very soon became clear that my stock had fallen to new depths, because I had only to step out of the back door to send Olly scurrying away into the fields. The situation became so bad that I began to brood about it.

"Helen," I said one morning, "this thing with Olly is getting on my nerves. I wish there was something I could do about it."

"There is, Jim," she said. "You'll really have to get to know him. And he'll have to get to know you."

I gave her a glum look. "I'm afraid that if you asked him, he'd tell you that he knows me only too well."

"Oh, I know, but when you think about it, over all the years that we've had these cats, they've hardly seen anything of you, except in an emergency. I've been the one to feed them, talk to them, pet them—day in, day out. They know me and trust me."

"That's right, but I just haven't had the time."

"Of course you haven't. Your life is one long rush. You're no sooner in the house than you're out again."

I nodded thoughtfully. She was so right. Over the years I had been attached to those cats, enjoyed the sight of them trotting down the slope for their food, playing in the long grass in the field, being fondled by Helen; but I was a comparative stranger to them. I felt a pang at the realisation that all that time had flashed past so quickly.

"Well, probably it's too late. Do you think there is anything I can do?"

"Yes," she said. "You have to start feeding them. You'll just have to find the time to do it. Oh, I know you can't do it always, but if there's the slightest chance, you'll have to get out there with their food."

"So you think it's just a case of cupboard love with them?"

"Absolutely not. I'm sure you've seen me with them often enough. They won't look at their food until I've made a fuss of them for quite a long time. It's the attention and friendship they want most."

"But I haven't a hope. They hate the sight of me."

"You'll just have to persevere. It took me a long time to get their trust. Especially with Ginny. She's always been the more timid one. Even now, if I move my hand too quickly, she's off. Despite all that's happened, I think Olly might be your best hope—there's a big well of friendliness in that cat."

"Right," I said. "Give me the food and milk. I'll start now."

That was the beginning of one of the little sagas in my life. At every opportunity, I was the one who called them down, placed the food on the wall top, and stood there waiting. At first I waited in vain. I could see the two of them watching me from the log shed—the black-and-white face and the yellow, gold, and white one observing me from the straw beds— and for a long time they would never venture down until I had retreated into the house. Because of my irregular job, it was difficult to keep the new system going; and sometimes when I had an early morning call, they didn't get their breakfast on time. But it was on one of those occasions when breakfast was over an hour late that their hunger overcame their fear and they came down cautiously while I stood stock stiff by the wall. They ate quickly with nervous glances at me, then scurried away. I smiled in satisfaction. It was the first breakthrough.

After that, there was a long period when I just stood there as they ate until they became used to me as part of the scenery. Then I tried a careful extension of a hand. To start with, they backed away at that; but as the days passed, I could see that my hand was becoming less and less of a threat, and my hopes rose steadily. As Helen had prophesied, Ginny was the one who shied right away from me at the slightest movement, whereas Olly, after retreating, began to look at me with an appraising eye as though he might possibly be willing to forget the past and revise his opinion of me. With infinite patience, day by day I managed to get my hand nearer and nearer to him, and it was a memorable occasion when he at last stood still and allowed me to touch his cheek with a forefinger. As I gently stroked the fur, he regarded me with unmistakably friendly eyes before skipping away.

"Helen," I said, looking round at the kitchen window, "I've made it! We're going to be friends at last. It's a matter of time now till I'm stroking him as you do." I was filled with an irrational pleasure and sense of fulfilment. It did seem a foolish reaction in a man who was dealing every day with animals of all kinds, but I was looking forward to years of friendship with that particular cat.

I was wrong. At that moment I could not have known that Olly would be dead within forty-eight hours.

It was the following morning when Helen called to me from the back garden. She sounded distraught. "Jim, come quickly! It's Olly!"

I rushed out to where she was standing, near the top of the slope close to the log shed. Ginny was there, but all I could see of Olly was a dark smudge on the grass.

Helen gripped my arm as I bent over him. "What's happened to him?"

He was motionless, his legs extended stiffly, his back arched in a dreadful rigor, his eyes staring.

"I . . . I'm afraid he's gone. It looks like strychnine poisoning." But as I spoke he moved slightly.

"Wait a minute!" I said. "He's still alive, but only just." I saw that the rigor had relaxed and I was able to flex his legs and lift him without any recurrence. "This isn't strychnine. It's like it, but it isn't. It's something cerebral, maybe a stroke."

Dry-mouthed, I carried him down to the house where he lay still, breathing almost imperceptibly.

Helen spoke through her tears. "What can you do?"

"Get him to the surgery right away. We'll do everything we can." I kissed her wet cheek and ran out to the car.

Siegfried and I sedated him because he had begun to make paddling movements with his limbs, then we injected him with steroids and antibiotics and put him on an intravenous drip. I looked at him as he lay in the big recovery cage, his paws twitching feebly. "Nothing more we can do, is there?"

Siegfried shook his head and shrugged. He agreed with me about the diagnosis—stroke, seizure, cerebral hemorrhage, call it what you like, but certainly the brain. I could see that he had the same feeling of hopelessness as I had.

We attended Olly all that day. I thought for a brief period during the afternoon that he was improving; but by evening he was comatose again, and he died during the night.

I brought him home, and as I lifted him from the car, his smooth, tangle-free fur was like a mockery now that his life was ended. I buried him just behind the log shed, a few feet from the straw bed where he had slept for so many years.

Vets are no different from other people when they lose a pet, and Helen and I were miserable. We hoped that the passage of time would dull our unhappiness, but we had another poignant factor to deal with. What about Ginny?

Those two cats had become a single entity in our lives, and we never thought of one without the other. It was clear that to Ginny the world was incomplete without Olly. For several days she ate nothing. We called her repeatedly; but she advanced only a few yards from the log house, looking around her in a puzzled way before turning back to her bed. For all those years, she had never trotted down that slope on her own; and over the next few weeks, her bewilderment as she gazed about her continually, seeking and searching for her companion, was one of the most distressing things we had ever had to witness.

Helen fed her in her bed for several days and eventually managed to coax her on to the wall, but Ginny could scarcely put her head down to the food without peering this way and that, still waiting for Olly to come and share it.

"She's so lonely," Helen said. "We'll have to try to make a bigger fuss of her now than ever. I'll spend more time outside talking with her, but if only we could get her inside with us. That would be the answer, but I know it will never happen."

I looked at the little creature, wondering if I'd ever get used to seeing only one cat on the wall; but Ginny sitting by the fireside or on Helen's knee was an impossible dream. "Yes, you're right, but maybe I can do something. I'd just managed to make friends with Olly—I'm going to start on Ginny now."

I knew I was taking on a long and maybe hopeless challenge because the tortoiseshell cat had always been the more timid of the two, but I pursued my purpose with resolution. At mealtimes and whenever I had the opportunity, I presented myself outside the back door, coaxing and wheedling, beckoning with my hand. For a long time, although she accepted the food from me, she would not let me near her. Then, maybe because she needed companionship so desperately that she felt she might as well even resort to me, the day came when she did not back away but allowed me to touch her cheek with my finger as I had done with Olly.

After that, progress was slow but steady. From touching I moved week by week to stroking her cheek, then to gently rubbing her ears, until finally I could run my hand the length of her body and tickle the root of her tail. From then on, undreamed-of familiarities gradually unfolded until she would not look at her food until she had paced up and down the wall top, again and again, arching herself in delight against my hand and brushing my shoulders with her body. Among these daily courtesies, one of her favourite ploys was to press her nose against mine and stand there for several moments looking into my eyes.

It was one morning several months later that Ginny and I were in this posture—she on the wall, touching noses with me, gazing into my eyes, drinking me in as though she thought I was rather wonderful and couldn't quite get enough of me— when I heard a sound from behind me.

"I was just watching the veterinary surgeon at work," Helen said softly.

"Happy work too," I said, not moving from my position, looking deeply into the green eyes—alight with friendship, fixed on mine a few inches away. "I'll have you know that this is one of my greatest triumphs."

Quiet Company

Lou Dean

Marvin. What an odd name for a cat. The woman at the shelter said he already had the name when they got him. "He's a little standoffish," she said. He was a big guy with gigantic paws—eight toes on each foot. "He'll be a good mouser," I said, and that's what I needed at my small farm up on Blue Mountain—not a cuddler.

Marvin fussed and flipped his yellow tail inside the carrier all the way home that summer day. I had a donkey and three Border collies, but Marvin would be my first cat. I lived alone—too alone sometimes, my friends claimed. They said I was overly independent, and there was some truth to that, but I was proud of my self-reliance.

"You'll like Blue Mountain, Marvin," I said as the cat and I pulled into the dirt drive. "Lots of mice around." His intense green eyes narrowed, and his giant paws clawed at the cage. *Let me out*, he seemed to say.

And out he went, the moment I released him. Marvin ran for the big elm tree next to my front porch and disappeared on the roof. From then on the roof became his favorite spot. He was a good mouser. And standoffish? Marvin was much more than that. For weeks I barely saw him, and at times I wondered if I still had a cat. The dry food and milk I put in the tool shed disappeared, so I knew he was around somewhere.

As summer faded into fall, Marvin made more frequent appearances. Drinking coffee on the porch, I'd spot his yellow tail flipping among the trees. "Morning, Marvin," I'd say. "How's the hunting?" He kept his distance. I knew the feeling. Still, I wished he'd let me stroke him once in a while.

Marvin liked my garden. While I bent over pumpkins pulling weeds one morning, he played hide-and-seek. "Gotcha!" I said, reaching for him. He scampered away, but came back, sneaking up behind the green beans. His game made the work easier. I talked to him, and he whisked his tail and fell on his back. He had a life of his own, that was obvious. I wasn't sure what part I had in it.

My donkey played hide-and-seek with Marvin too, but the dogs chased him mercilessly. One day, when I latched the kennel gate, Marvin appeared. "Your turn," I said. He strolled nonchalantly just outside the fenced area, and rolled in the grass with a look of satisfaction. The dogs barked and jumped, but they could do nothing. Marvin had his revenge. I laughed until my sides ached.

I fell hopelessly in love with my mouser. Sometimes I reached out to caress him, but he quickly jumped back. I told myself to be patient. But I wasn't patient, not really. I wanted to know I had Marvin's love in return.

One summer, when I broke my ankle, my outside activity was greatly restricted. Marvin disappeared, and I missed him terribly. I spent hours hobbling around on crutches in the yard, calling his name. My friends searched the barn, the fields, and the road ditches. They were happy to help because I so rarely asked them for anything. Two months after he'd gone missing, I wept for Marvin at night, loudly and mournfully, knowing only God could hear.

My friend Brenda came over to keep me company one weekend. "I feel silly getting this worked up over a cat," I confessed to her, "but I thought the two of us had a real bond."

"Maybe you're not as independent as you make yourself out to be, Lou Dean. That's okay, you know."

It wouldn't be the first time an animal taught me something. Living with a donkey had shown me I was as stubborn as he was. God had surprised me with that lesson. *Lord, I guess Brenda is right.* Everybody needed to be cuddled once in a while. Everybody except Marvin, that is.

Brenda hugged me goodbye. I thumped to the edge of the porch on my crutches to see her off. Halfway down the sidewalk, she turned to wave. "There's Marvin!" she said. "On the roof. Only one cat has paws like that."

I almost broke my other ankle getting off the porch. The cat was thin and straggly, but he was definitely Marvin. He looked at me with those intense green eyes, his yellow tail flipping. I warmed some milk and opened a can of tuna. I hobbled to the porch. "Marvin?" I called. He devoured the tuna, then lapped up the milk as I sat on the steps. "Did you get locked in a barn somewhere?" I asked. "I worried and cried. I thought you were gone forever."

Marvin strolled over and lifted his giant paws. I couldn't believe what was happening. He gently felt my face all over with his paws. After five years on Blue Mountain, we'd finally touched. I knew that wherever he'd been, he'd come back to be with me.

We were two loners who loved each other's company. I spent quiet times every evening in the garden just so I could visit with my cat. Sometimes he was out hunting, but he would always come. He would jump in my lap and put his paws on my face. That woman in the shelter wouldn't have recognized Marvin—or me.

We were together for twelve years. When he developed kidney failure, the vet said there was only one humane choice. I found a place near the garden where we'd had our quiet times. I placed flat rocks over the grave, and knelt beside it. "Thank you, Lord, for Marvin, who softened my heart." I felt the slightest touch on my face. Not paws exactly. It was something even more comforting than Marvin's requited love—God's.

The Purr

of an Angel

Rock, Bach,
and Sweets

Katy Jenkin

One Saturday morning when the phone rang, I rushed past my son's bedroom to answer. Lucky I even heard it, I thought. Sixteen-year-old Tony had taken up the electric guitar and drums, and his hard rock sometimes drowned out other sounds and conversations. For months his dad and I had argued with Tony about his music, and I was reaching the end of my rope. I couldn't stand the racket, I couldn't stand the lyrics, and I was worried about the influence that kind of music might have on my son. My constant prayer was for peace and quiet.

But at that moment, in a turmoil, I picked up the phone. It was my friend Kathleen, who was preparing to move to England. "I just found out that I can't take Sweets with me," she said. Sweets, her gray tabby cat of eight years, meant the world to Kathleen. "If I can't find a home for her, I don't know what will happen. Would you consider taking her in?"

Without warning, a yellow flash zipped across the countertop and landed in the butter dish. Our new kitten, Missy, had struck again. "Get out of there!" I yelled. Then Princess, our German shepherd, sauntered into the kitchen and cocked her head at me as if she understood my dilemma. I already had two pets. Could I handle a third? Kathleen waited for my response. "I'll think about it," I told her, hanging up the phone and surveying the butter tracks on the kitchen floor. At that moment Tony's music started upstairs again. My teeth clenched. It would be impossible to add another element to this circus.

And yet the idea nagged at me. When I broached the idea of a new cat sharing our space, my husband and son said they wouldn't mind. Once again I was going through my mental list of all the reasons why not to take Sweets when it occurred to me the decision wasn't entirely on my shoulders. "Dear God, what should I do?" I asked. Something told me to say yes.

I called Kathleen with the good news. "Oh, thank you so much, Katy. I know you two will be fast friends," she said. Then she reeled off Sweets's quirks: "She loves broccoli and classical music and—"

"Classical music?"

"Yes, believe it or not," Kathleen said. "It calms her. She purrs when it's playing."

On the day of Kathleen's departure, Tony and I went to pick up Sweets. Kathleen tearfully hugged her cat goodbye, then gave a last-minute admonition to my son: "Don't forget the classical music!"

On the arrival of Sweets at our house, Missy and Princess sniffed the cat carrier and started hissing and barking. "Hey, Mom, Sweets can stay with me," Tony said. Before I could stop him, he hurried upstairs, carrying Sweets to her "safe" environment. Left to calm our pets downstairs, I didn't have the energy to intervene. I shuddered, thinking of my son's room, complete with drums, electric guitars, and amplifiers. I just didn't see how this could end without more discord.

The next morning Tony rushed off to school after a brief announcement that the night had gone well for Sweets. "Don't let her out of my room, Mom," he warned. "I have it all set up for her."

Of course I had to open the door a crack to check for myself. I couldn't believe my ears. Strains of Bach floated out to greet me. An obviously contented Sweets was perched next to the radio, purring away. My son, the rock music fan, had set his radio to a classical station! I didn't realize Tony knew such music existed.

Evenings passed with Tony doing math homework to the strains of Rachmaninoff. Mornings began not with electric guitars but with violins. As the days went on, rock selections still emitted from the room from time to time, but more and more there were concertos, sonatas and symphonies.

The other animals settled down; and as I did my morning chores, we all enjoyed the sound of Haydn drifting from Tony's room.

God had answered my prayer by bringing harmony to the whole household. He had sent Sweets, the cat who craved classical music.

A Black-Cat Tale

Barbara Billingsley Mohler

Sometimes, as the saying goes, there's the last straw. And then sometimes there's the last cat! The time of the last cat had come to our household. Our latest housecat, Pajamas, had disappeared, and when it became clear that he'd never return, I said to my two youngest children, "That's it, kids. No replacement. No more cats."

My declaration may have seemed cold-hearted, but I felt I had good grounds. Cats had brought me nothing but trials. Judy, Bounce, Little Angel, Quigley, Duffy . . . I was tired of the whole thing. As a single parent with young children, I had enough to worry about. I didn't need to be dashing to the grocery store for pet food or combing the area at midnight for another wayward tabby. I'd had it. No more cats!

Well, I repeated my declaration until I was nearly blue in the face, and still Sherman, then ten, and Ginger, seven, wouldn't give up their hopes. A month went by and they never failed to make me aware of whose cats in the area had had kittens. And it appeared that practically every family had kittens to spare.

Finally I came up with one of my bright ideas. "Kids," I

said, "let's pray about it and lay a fleece before the Lord." They avidly agreed.

By saying "fleece," I was of course invoking the example of Gideon's fleece, from Judges 6:36–40. In that passage, Gideon asks God, as a sign of assurance, to soak a fleece with dew while the ground all around remains dry. And the Lord did just that. It shames me a little to say so, but I think I made a deliberately outlandish request.

"Lord," I prayed, "the children feel that we should have a cat. I disagree, so we are coming to you for direction. Father, if we are to have a cat, I am asking you to have a kitty walk up our pathway straight to our door. Amen."

"And, Lord," added Ginger, "please make him black." Her addition didn't worry me. By now I was sure my prayer was sufficiently unanswerable.

More than a month went by. No cat. I figured I was in the clear . . . until the day I walked across the street to visit with a friend. As I rang her doorbell—with my back turned to my own house—I heard hysterically gleeful cries behind me.

"Mom, Mom, Mom! Look, look, look!"

I turned to look back. There, wobbling up my pathway, was a tiny kitty. A black kitty, no less. The Word of God says "faint not." I tried not to. The kids started jumping up and down. "Thank you, Jesus," they cried.

My friend opened her door just as the black kitty walked through my door. "I can't believe this," she laughed, having learned earlier of my ruse. "That's the Lord's cat."

And so he was . . . and still is at age eleven. Named

"Meow-buddy," he has never run away, never gotten stuck in trees, never clawed my upholstery, and is, most amazingly, agreeable to any and all kinds of cat food. I guess you could call our black cat golden.

Theodora,
God's Gift

JoLynne Waltz

Several months ago I moved eight hundred miles away from my family to start my first job after college. I loved my work. But coming home to the emptiness of the apartment I'd rented was no fun.

Early one morning I was awakened by the meowing of a cat—and it was close. I got up to investigate. In the kitchen I found the back door open—I was certain I'd locked it the night before—and, to my amazement, there was a tattered, green-eyed tiger cat striding imperiously around the room. Quickly I made a search of the apartment. Nothing was missing; nothing had been tampered with. Reassured, but puzzled, I knelt to pet the cat. She nuzzled against me, purring contentedly.

A few days passed. No one in the neighborhood claimed her, and no one advertised for a lost cat. By that time it would have been hard to give her up—we clearly enjoyed each other's company.

"I guess it's safe to name you, my friend," I told her. "I'm going to call you Theodora."

That night, during my weekly phone call home, I told my mother about my new four-footed roommate.

"I'm glad you have a pet, JoLynne." she said. "I've been worried about you being so lonely. In fact, I've been praying about it every day." And then she chuckled. "Where ever did you get that name—Theodora"

"I don't know. Mom. It just came to me out of nowhere, the way she did."

What neither of us knew then was the derivation of the name "Theodora." It's from the Greek: *Theo*, "God"; *dora*, "gift." Theodora—the cat, like her name—God's gift!

Daddy's Last Days

Jane Jordan Heinrich

My daddy was a high school football star, the highest scorer in the state, and later a halfback for Texas Christian University. He was even offered a spot on the Chicago Bears, but he turned it down, preferring a quiet life with Mama and us two kids, and working with his hands every day, fixing electronics in his shop. After retirement he specialized in restoring antique televisions and radios. I used to love watching Daddy at his worktable, repairing some vintage machine, his big, calloused hands moving so carefully among those thin wires. He had the same gentle touch with people. Daddy was able to cheer me up with a wink or an I-love-you smile, or comfort me with a squeeze of his hand.

When Daddy was diagnosed with cancer in an advanced stage, I felt like the rug had been pulled out from under me. He was ninety-one years old, and I knew it was time to let him go. But as the disease stole away his strength and made him so weak that he could barely move or talk, I longed to make him feel as safe and secure in his last days as he'd always made me feel.

We put Daddy in hospice care. Mama, my brother, Bob, and I checked him in that first day. Mama set up flowers and plants in the private room, Bob lined family photos on Dad's bedside table where he could see them easily, and I slipped an extra pillow under his head. He stared out the window so fixedly, I wasn't even sure he knew we were in the room.

"I don't know if any of this helps, Daddy," I whispered to him, touching his outstretched hand. "I just wish you could tell me what you need." He squeezed my fingers with a familiar firmness, and our eyes met for a moment. Then his gaze lost focus and drifted away. Something brushed my leg, and I looked down. Sitting at my feet was a plump gray and white tabby cat. She looked up at me, eyes closing in a friendly cat-smile, then rubbed her soft, furry side against my leg.

"That must be the cat the nurse at the front desk was telling us about," Mama said, bending down to scratch her under the chin. "Her name is Hope."

"She lives here?" I asked. Bob picked the cat up and laid her carefully on the bed at Daddy's feet.

"For some time now. Apparently she has a way with sick people," he said.

Hope glanced at Daddy, then made her way purposefully up the sheets, lay down beside his legs, and began purring. A smile crept over the tired lines of Daddy's face. "Looks like she's made a new friend," Mama said.

For the rest of the day, Hope hardly left Daddy's side. She lay curled in a gray ball on his legs as Mama, Bob, and I sat by the bed. We read and talked to Daddy, and at first he seemed to understand. His eyes would even fill sometimes with that good humor we knew so well. But after a while he seemed to drift away, staring at the window or the wall.

By the end of the day, we'd all fallen into silence, watching the light grow dimmer through the window. The only sounds in the room were Daddy's slow breathing and Hope's purr, steady and gentle beneath it.

That first night, I stayed with Daddy. Bob had to work in the morning, and Mama was worn out from the long day. I lay awake in the bed next to Daddy's, listening to him breathe. Staring into the darkness, I saw our whole life together: Daddy holding me as a baby, teaching me how to swim, how to dance, how to make a garden grow.

Daddy used to pick wildflowers by the hundreds and dry them for their seeds. These he carried in his pockets everywhere he went, and he scattered them by the handful wherever he found a bare patch of earth. I remembered my first day of school, how upset I had been at the thought of leaving him and Mama. But on the bus ride there, I'd seen bright yellow patches of Daddy's wildflowers all along the roadside, and I felt like he was still with me.

Now, as I lay beside Daddy in the darkness, it was those little things that I remembered in such great detail. Did he know how much they'd meant to me, how close to him they'd made me feel? I fell asleep that night wishing I could tell him and know that he'd understand.

The next day, Daddy's condition was worse. His face was pale, and he looked at us with a blank, uncomprehending gaze. On the morning of the third day, he had a fit of trembling in his arms and legs that was so intense it shook the bed. I crawled in beside him and wrapped his body in my arms to stop the shaking. *Dear Lord, help me comfort him.* Hope jumped onto the bed and, with gentle insistence, nestled a space for herself between us. She propped her front paws on Daddy's stomach and brushed her tail against me.

After the trembling stopped, I returned to my bed. I'd always felt so safe when Daddy held me wrapped in his strong arms. It seemed impossible that this frail figure sleeping in the bed beside me could be the same man.

I turned onto my side, burying my face in the pillow, and tears sprang into my eyes. After a moment, something soft brushed against my nose, and I looked up. Hope had jumped onto the bed beside me, her silent warmth soothing my sorrow.

Daddy passed in and out of consciousness the whole next day, and I wondered with each breath he took if it would be his last. That night, I shut out the lights, feeling emotionally and physically drained. But as soon as my head touched the pillow, I felt a soft weight beside me. Almost every night after that, Hope slept in the bed beside me.

On the fifth day, Daddy's breathing became labored and erratic. Mama, Bob, and I gathered around his bed. From her spot at his feet, Hope raised her head and perked up her ears. She seemed to study Daddy's face, then stood and padded quietly to his shoulder. She laid her head on the pillow by his ear and began to purr. Within minutes his breathing became peaceful again.

Mama was so shaken by that close call that she had to leave the room and sit in the hall. Hope got up from her place on Daddy's pillow and followed her. As soon as I was sure his breathing had lapsed back to normal, I went to the door and looked out. Mama was holding Hope in her lap, pressing her face against the cat's soft fur, murmuring into her ear. Even as I watched, I could see the pain and heartache ease out of Mama's face.

After seven days in hospice care, Daddy fell into a deep, untroubled sleep from which we knew he wouldn't wake. We sat around his bed the last day, holding his hand and saying prayers.

Hope did not leave Daddy's hospice room once that day, not even to eat. We stroked her where she lay at Daddy's side, peacefully purring. And as we waited, that steady sound seemed to fill the room. When Daddy finally left this world, slipping easily from sleep, Hope continued to purr in his lap, soft as a whisper, until even she was quiet.

That spring, every road I drove down in our little town seemed to be lined with Daddy's wildflowers. They poked their yellow heads from empty lots and friends' gardens, brighter than they'd ever been before. And whenever I saw them I thought about the last week Daddy and I had spent together.

Somehow, I felt sure that I had been able to comfort Daddy in the little ways that matter most, and that he had understood all the things I'd wanted to say to him. I think that was because Hope was there, passing between us. She knew exactly what we all needed. It was as simple as being together.

Dharma, the Cat
Who Took Away Fear

Debbie Blais

Wrapping my arms across my chest, I set out for the two-block walk to the lake. I was tired and weak, but I needed to get out of the house and clear my head in the cool September air. Three months earlier, in June 1995, I had been diagnosed with breast cancer. After undergoing a radical mastectomy, I thought the worst was behind me; but the cancer had spread to my lymph nodes. Now I was part of an aggressive clinical-research trial that included a combination of high-dose chemotherapy and hormone-blocking drugs aimed at destroying the cancer cells and preventing a recurrence. I was thirty-seven and terrified of dying. Nightmares plagued me when I lay down to sleep.

The long, twice-monthly chemo treatments wiped me out completely for days at a stretch. Keeping down bread and water was next to impossible. My hair fell out in clumps. I suffered these side effects almost willingly. But after a particularly draining treatment that week, I had run a dangerously high fever. Death was closing in on me, and I wondered if there was any escape.

A wind blew and I reached up to keep my cap from

flying off and exposing my bald head. Walking to the lake on balmy fall afternoons used to delight me, but now the way the clouds moved together and apart, the leaves fluttering in circles on the breeze, only reminded me of what I'd miss when I was gone.

I stopped at the edge of the lake and stared down at the sandy bottom. *Why is this happening, God?* A high-pitched mewling sounded from a nearby bush. I was familiar with that cry, having rescued many a stray kitten.

I can't help you, I thought sadly. *I can barely take care of myself.* I'd gotten a medical leave from my job, and my husband Gary had taken over caring for our three cats and doing most of the housework after putting in full days at his carpentry business.

"Meow! Meow!" the pleas continued. I closed my eyes tight. Ear-splitting shrieks and squawks filled the air. I whirled around. Four blue jays were swooping down upon the bush. I shooed the birds away and carefully pulled back the tangled branches. A tiny orange tabby with bright blue eyes peered up at me, mewling like a baby. I couldn't just leave him there. I gently picked him up and held him in my palm.

"Little one, I don't know which of us is in worse shape," I said, running my fingers through the shivering kitten's fur. *Maybe Gary could find him a home.* I walked back to the house and collapsed on the couch. The kitty curled up on my chest, near the scar from my operation. For hours I stroked him and his purring calmed me.

"What do we have here?" Gary asked, smiling, when he came home from work.

"You know what a sucker I am for hard-luck cases," I said. "Would you take him around and see if someone wants him?"

After Gary left with the kitten, I lay down on the couch and stared at the second hand on the clock, which was moving slowly, imperturbably around the face. Our three cats sat on the windowsill watching the deepening twilight. I found myself missing the little ball of softness that had nestled on my chest all afternoon. Finally I paged my husband. "Do you still have the kitty?" I asked when he called.

"I was just about to give him to someone."

"Don't. I need him."

When Gary brought the kitty back, he curled up on my chest again as if it were home.

The following morning the kitten purred me awake, and for the next few days he was with me around the clock. He loved to snuggle his face under my chin.

"What am I going to name you?" I said one night, looking down at him. He seemed to have found his place comforting me. "Is that what you're here for?" I asked, scratching the back of his neck. "Is that your purpose?" I'd read once that "dharma" is a Hindu term meaning one's purpose or place in life. "I'll call you Dharma," I decided, looking him in the eyes. *What about me, God?* I wondered. *What's my purpose?* For the time being, all I wanted was to give this kitten as much love as he was giving me.

I spent the days reading, listening to inspirational tapes,

and participating in cancer support groups on the Internet, with Dharma never far away. When I was exhausted, Dharma nuzzled my cheek and kept me going. He brought out in me a spirit of fun and whimsy that for months my fears had stifled. "Kiss me, Dharma," I'd say, planting one on his nose.

As he grew, he got to running through the house, clawing furniture. Shortly after one chemo treatment, I lay on the couch, weary and bored. Dharma climbed onto the armrest and began scratching it to shreds. "I think we've both got cabin fever," I told him. I brought him out to our backyard, where the other cats were playing. A flutter of yellow wings passed overhead. Dharma pawed at the air and began chasing the butterfly about the garden. His joy was infectious. I sat on the steps and laughed as he leaped and meowed among the hibiscus and jasmine and long-stemmed purple Porter's weed. Watching him made me feel like I didn't have a care in the world. And to think that at first I hadn't wanted to keep him!

After my last treatment in November, my doctor told me I was cancer-free. Finally I could tune back into the world.

As my strength slowly returned, I spent less time on the couch and more time on the back steps watching Dharma chase the elusive butterflies. I also started doing more house-work. I carried Dharma like a baby to the garage with me when I did the laundry and let him tag along when I vacu-umed, his purring almost as loud as the whirring motor. "Not fair. You have a little helper," Gary joked. "I had to clean up alone." In December I had reconstructive surgery and made plans to return to work.

Three days after the surgery, I opened the back door to let the cats into the backyard to play. Just before I let Dharma go, I scooped him up and said, "Oh, I love you so much," kissing him as usual. He pressed his nose against my lips, kissing me back! I watched him scamper off after a butterfly before I went back inside to take a nap. Scenes of Dharma romping with the butterflies filled my mind. My dreams were much more pleasant these days.

I awoke around dusk to the sound of the doorbell. I got up and saw Gary talking to a neighbor at the door. She handed him something wrapped in a blanket. I glimpsed a tuft of orange fur peeking out of its folds.

Dharma!

Somehow he had gotten out of the backyard and been hit by a car. I couldn't believe it. "No, no," I kept saying, feeling somehow that if I said it enough, Dharma would not be lost to that great unknown that haunted me. Gary laid him down in the garden. Then he put his arms around me. "You know, Debbie," he said softly, "I think God sent you this angel to help you through a very rough time. Now that his job's done, God's brought him home."

I thought about Gary's words as he dug a small grave for Dharma near the Porter's weed. Sitting on the back steps in the cool dusk, I could still see Dharma, a blur of orange traipsing through the flowers, and felt at peace even in the midst of my grief. I knew the memories he gave me would be with me always. On the tiny headstone I wrote by hand, "Dharma, my little angel."

He had inspired me to seek life's joy when I was at my lowest. Today, nearly three years later, not only am I cancer-free, I am also free of my paralyzing fear of death. I live each day to the utmost, as Dharma taught me, and trust God to take care of the rest.

One Lucky Cat

Donna Francis

A week after Smokey, our family's barn cat, prematurely delivered a litter of kittens, my mother called to tell me that all but one of the kittens had died. Mom moved Smokey and her remaining kitten into the garage and promised to keep me posted. A couple of weeks later, Mom called again. She said that something was wrong with the remaining kitten, and Dad wanted to "put him out of his misery." Since I have a lot of experience volunteering for my local SPCA (Society for the Prevention of Cruelty to Animals), Mom asked me to take a look at the kitten and tell her what I thought about his health.

When I arrived at my parents' home, I saw something unusual. Smokey was nursing a small, mouselike, three-week-old gray tabby kitten. The kitten had only one eye open, and his mouth was deformed. With a crooked stub of a tail and a drunken walk, he was much more uncoordinated than most kittens his age.

Although I was concerned about this kitten's tiny size and premature condition, I couldn't help noticing that he was a real character. Whenever he heard our human voices, he would leave his feline mom and seek us out. He followed us everywhere as fast as he could with his lurching walk. If any-one picked him up, he purred immediately. The tiny kitten seemed so happy that I convinced my parents to give him another week.

The next weekend, I drove back to my parents' home expecting to find that the kitten had deteriorated. He had indeed lost some weight, but he still showed the zest for life I'd seen in him the week before. I asked my parents to let me take the kitten home with me so that I could put him in with a group of orphaned kittens I was fostering for the SPCA. I made the offer with the stipulation that I would not keep the kitten; I already had two dogs and a cantankerous Persian cat who hated other male cats.

The week after I brought the kitten to my apartment, we visited the veterinarian. There, I was surprised to learn that not only was this kitten underweight, but the formula he'd been eating was causing him respiratory problems. The vet gave me suggestions on how to quickly graduate him to eating dry food. The vet also explained that this kitten had a cleft palate and nose and should have died at birth or shortly there-after; kittens with this type of deformity usually can't nurse properly. The vet checked the kitten's closed eye and said that it would never open. The entire left side of this kitten's face had not developed, and his staggering walk suggested that he might have brain damage. The prognosis for the little guy was not good. The vet predicted that the kitten would not live past his first birthday.

I cried on the way home from the veterinarian's office.

What am I doing? I wondered. *Does this kitten have any chance at all?*

When I came home, I put the kitten in the bathroom in a place I'd set up for the foster kittens. These babies were the kitten's age—four weeks old—yet he was only half their size and not nearly as well developed. With sadness in my heart, I wondered if the kindest thing would be to let my vet put this tiny, deformed creature to sleep. I went into the kitchen to cook dinner and think about what I should do.

As I made dinner, I noticed that Abbie, my toy poodle, wasn't underfoot as she usually is at dinnertime. I went to see what trouble she might be up to and was shocked by what I found. I had isolated the kittens from the rest of my four-legged family with a tall baby gate in the bathroom doorway. In the three years I'd been fostering kittens, the permanent residents of my household and the foster kittens had remained safely separated. However, I found Abbie staring intently at the baby gate. To my surprise, with one giant leap she jumped over it to where the kittens were. I had no fear of her harming them, but I'd never seen her show any interest in the foster kitties. I silently watched as Abbie went straight to the deformed kitten and gently picked him up by the scruff of his neck. She climbed back over the baby gate with the kitten in her mouth and took him to my bed. There, she snuggled with the kitten and groomed him.

After a few minutes of tenderly caring for the kitten, Abbie looked up at me as if to say, *If you don't want to take care of him, I will. I won't give up on him.* I guess you could say that, in that instant, Abbie made up my mind for me. The kitten was here to stay.

I never again isolated the kitten with the foster kittens; Abbie wouldn't allow it. If I tried to take the kitten to the bathroom, Abbie would grab him and carry him to my bed. (Not a good thing, since this little kitten wasn't litter-trained yet.) Abbie and the little kitten became inseparable; she took over his care and even protected him from my other cat.

In the meantime, my foster kittens were getting adopted and new foster kittens were arriving. No one who arrived as a prospective adopter seemed to be interested in a one-eyed, deformed kitten with breathing problems. Okay, so maybe I didn't try as hard as I could to find him a home, but I couldn't bring myself to upset Abbie by adopting out her baby.

Due to the respiratory problems caused by his cleft palate and nose, I had to take the kitten to the vet several times a month. At one point, he was even going to the vet twice a day for treatments. Each night, Abbie and I closed ourselves in the bathroom with the kitten and a vaporizer, just so this baby could breathe. Many nights I cried, fearing for the poor creature's life. I would listen to the kitten struggling for breath and wonder if it was cruel to keep him alive. But all I had to do was look into Abbie's eyes as she expressed her love for him, and I knew I was doing the right thing. *Don't give up on our baby*, Abbie seemed to be saying. Our dedication was fueled by the mischievous sparkle that lingered in the kitten's eye.

Months after his arrival, I still had not named the kitten. This was partly to spare my feelings. I kept thinking, *I can't bear to name a kitten who might not survive.* I had been through the pain of having foster kittens die, and I was not looking forward to feeling that kind of loss again.

With the vet's help and constant advice, we eventually got the kitten's breathing problems under control. I was delighted when he could go for an entire month without treatments. Finally, he was healthy enough to be neutered. On the day of the surgery, I realized that the perfect name for this kitten was Lucky. Yet I still had my doubts about what kind of life a sickly, deformed kitten would have. I needn't have worried.

As I write this story, Lucky is six and a half years old and weighs a healthy—even portly—sixteen pounds. Fortunately, he has no brain damage at all. But when he sleeps by my head at night, it sounds like I'm with Darth Vader. Lucky's cleft palate makes him snore louder than most humans do. I don't mind. Lucky still has that special swagger in his walk. My Persian cat didn't grow to love Lucky, but he never tried to beat him up, as he had the other male cats I'd brought home. And, much to my amazement, this very special cat who had such a rough start in life has grown up to be an award-winning therapy cat.

I started taking Lucky to work with me at Jefferson Elementary School in Sherman, Texas, where I taught deaf children. There he began to share duties with Abbie, who is a registered therapy dog.

When Lucky came to school, he would greet everyone at the door with a loud "Meow!" If that didn't get my students' attention, Lucky would paw at their legs until they said hello or petted him. Then he'd sprawl out on the table and bask in the children's attention. My students loved it when Lucky decided that they'd worked long enough; he'd lie right down in the middle of their work. We called this "taking a Lucky break."

When Lucky purred, it excited my deaf students; they didn't have to hear it to know that they were making him happy. They could feel the vibration of his purring with their fingers, and they could see him shake. Lucky shakes when he is happy—which is most of the time, as long as someone is giving him attention.

Lucky also worked with the hearing students. One year, we had a writing contest in a first-grade classroom. The children were to write a short story about the therapy pet of their choice. Several students chose to write about Lucky. One low-achieving student, who hardly ever finished his work, turned in a story that won first prize. He was very proud of his story, but not as proud as I was. In his story, he'd written: "I love Lucky because he loves me too."

Another of Lucky's volunteer jobs was at the Reba McEntire Center for Rehabilitation in Denison, Texas. He loved to lie on the clients' beds and feel their love. The clients and staff got a kick out of seeing a cat walking on a leash down the sterile halls of the center.

Lucky's deformities caused clients at the rehabilitation center to realize that their conditions could be worse. A client said, "Lucky reminds me of the saying 'I cried because I had no shoes; then I saw a man who had no feet.'" On one visit, a nurse came and got us out of a client's room; another client was upset because we'd skipped her room when she was asleep. By the time we arrived from the other end of the center, this client was out of bed and in her wheelchair, rolling down the hall to be sure she got to see Lucky. She took one long look at him and said "My goodness, he's worse off than we are."

But perhaps one of Lucky's most important jobs was to teach people about differences—either their own or other people's. I helped Lucky write his autobiography, which we still use to teach schoolchildren about accepting differences. I can only hope that the children learn the lesson Lucky lived to teach.

I didn't realize how effective Lucky and I were at conveying his message until the mother of one of my students related a story to me. This student was a beautiful little girl who was having trouble understanding why she was deaf and different from other kids. She would go home after Lucky's visits to our classroom and describe him and his antics to her father in detail. This was a wonderful way to expand her limited language skills, which was one of her educational goals. One day after she had described Lucky's visit, she said, "And he only has one eye. But that's okay, Daddy; he's different, just like me."

Lucky put in almost six years of hard, loving work before retiring due to the onset of carsickness. He isn't taking retirement well, as he now seems to feel neglected; I can't give him all the attention his clients used to give him.

Yet I think that Lucky has used up at least four of his nine lives. Looking back on Lucky's career, I'm amazed at how successful he was. In October 2000, Lucky was the co-winner of Delta Society's National Therapy Pet of the Year Award. Lucky and I flew to Boston to receive the award, and he was the only cat present. Highlights of Lucky's life story have appeared in newspapers, magazines (*Animal Wellness*, *Cat Fancy*, *Cats*, and *Pet Life*), and a book (*The Healing Power of Pets*, by Dr. Marty Becker). He was also featured in a segment of *Amazing Animals* on the Animal Planet network and on *Miracle Pets* on the PAX network. Lucky's photo even appears in the *2003 Cat-a-Day Calendar*. Lucky not only worked miracles; his entire life is a miracle. Lucky continues to inspire people to never let misfortunes or obstacles keep them from giving their best to life.

Mahgy

Mary Beninghoff

Mahgy (sounds like "doggy") is my cat. I met her at a no-kill pet shelter in Chicago in 1988, six months after I had lost my feline companion of more than twenty years, Fat Baby. I had stopped in to leave a donation in Fat Baby's memory, and I was talked into looking at their resident cats. I had sworn I'd never have another pet (famous last words), but I agreed.

The kittens were adorable, but they said that I would have to take two. It was a rule of theirs intended to keep the kittens from being lonely. I decided that since I was there, I would go upstairs to look at the adult cats, knowing I wouldn't be tempted by a grown animal (more famous last words).

I was intrigued by a small black cat lying on top of an introduction cage. Every time I reached for it, I was greeted with hisses and growls. When I turned to look at the others, however, I felt a tap on my back. When I turned back, the cat had moved closer to me, but it still growled. This happened three times, and I finally asked the attendant about the belligerent little feline.

Her name was Mahogany, and she had been found about a year ago. She had crawled into the engine of a car, trying to get warm, and she had cuts on her hip and had obviously been abused. She was about two and a half years old when they found her and about three and a half when I met her. She'd been adopted three times but had been returned for biting, and she was now labeled "unadoptable."

There was something so appealing in her eyes that I couldn't resist. I told them I would take her. After trying to persuade me not to, two attendants got her downstairs for the vet to examine her, and it took two more to put her into the carrier for her trip home.

When I opened the box at my apartment, my new cat bolted under the bed and I didn't see her again for weeks. She ate and used her litter box, so I knew she was all right, but no amount of coaxing could get her out from under the bed. I figured it was okay. We were two old maids living together, and she could have her space and I would have mine. At least she was safe, and it felt good to have another living being in the apartment.

I was reading one evening, almost three weeks later, when I saw her little head sticking out from under the dust ruffle. I started reading out loud. She watched me for an hour. When I got up, she retreated. This went on every night for a week or so until one evening she came out and sat by the bed about four feet from me. I continued to read, and I inserted the name I had given her into the reading. I had shortened Mahogany to Mahgy, trying to get her used to the sound.

Two months to the day after I brought her home, she startled us both by jumping onto the arm of my chair. She was only there a few seconds, but I felt we'd made a breakthrough. After that, for another month, she would sit on the chair arm and watch me when I read to her. She looked up when I said Mahgy.

One evening, instead of settling on the arm, she crawled into the space between the chair arm and my leg and stretched out full length. I was still hesitant to touch her, remembering her previous reaction, so I waited for her move. It came when she got on the bed with me one night and stretched out along my back. We had made it.

The first time I touched her, she tensed and then relaxed as I stroked her gently. About four months from our meeting, I could finally pick her up and take her to Fat Baby's vet, Dr. Rubin, a well-known cat expert who often appears on Oprah Winfrey's show. Mahgy was so good in the car. She relaxed beside me on the seat and again in the doctor's office, and the doctor said she had obviously been cared for at one time. When he examined her mouth, however, Dr. Rubin became furious. The shelter had obviously not checked her teeth. She had gingivitis so bad that her gums were bleeding. Her teeth were broken and several were loose and ready to come out. He said it was no wonder she was a biter and belligerent. She must have been in constant pain.

Over the next six months, the doctor removed five molars and several broken teeth. He used a tranquilizer to be able to deep-clean her gums and remaining teeth. The change in her personality was miraculous. The vet said she had to have been in agony, especially when she tried to eat the dry food at the shelter. I had fed her canned food, because that's what Fat Baby had eaten, and the doctor said it probably saved her life. He had no doubt she would have slowly starved on the dry food.

Within six months, Mahgy became a beautiful and loving companion. The only things she objected to were having her feet touched and claws clipped and having her belly rubbed. The doctor felt she may have had frostbite at one time, and her feet were probably painful when touched. She had learned to protect her belly when she was on the street.

I retired from my job in Chicago in 1995 and moved back to Indiana, my home. Mahgy had never seen anything bigger than a rat or pigeon in Chicago; but on our first night in our new home, we were greeted by about thirty ducks parading past our patio. My apartment overlooked government-protected wetlands, and wildlife teemed. I have a picture of Mahgy studying the ducks, standing as still as a statue as they paused on the patio. The ducks didn't really bother her, but the small birds flitting around drove her nuts. And when the little mouse made its appearance, I thought she would go through the screen. I bought a baby gate to protect the screen door. Life was good.

Naturally I had to find a new doctor for myself. When I did, he decided to try to get my diabetes under better control, and he put me on a new medication along with the insulin. It worked beautifully until the day Mahgy had to save my life.

I had gotten up that morning feeling rather sluggish and not well. I took the insulin, then ate a light breakfast and sat down to read the newspaper. It was cool in early November, so I covered myself with a soft throw and fell asleep.

I woke up two hours later with something pounding on my face and chest. When I opened my eyes, Mahgy was sitting on my chest, batting at my face and chest with her paws. I felt rotten. My first thought was my blood sugar. When I tested, the reading was 36 instead of the normal 120.

I immediately loaded up on orange juice and peanut butter, and an hour later I checked again. It was higher and I felt better.

When I told my doctor about it later, he said if the reading had been a few points lower, I could have fallen into a coma. He guessed that Mahgy had sensed that my breathing was different and reacted. For whatever reason she did it, I was grateful and sure that she had paid me back for any care I had given her.

But she wasn't through yet. A month later, the same thing happened. It was so sudden, I didn't realize I was falling asleep. Again Mahgy pounded my face and body until I awoke. The reading was 46 that day.

We immediately adjusted my medication, and I have had no further problems with it. I will always be grateful for whatever made me choose Mahgy in spite of the many reasons not to. She has proven to be not only a marvelous companion, but a caring and resourceful friend as well.

I've never regretted choosing her and we are now growing old, not too gracefully, together. I'm seventy and she will soon be seventeen. We're both slowing down, but life is good. We have each other.

Golden Star Lost

Garnet Hunt White

Golden Star didn't come for his food that early August morning. Where could he be? Glenn, my husband, called until his voice became gravelly: "Golden Star! Kitty! Kitty! Golden Star!"

I called and called until I lost my voice. Then I taped the calls and set the recorder on the porch.

Glenn, our dog Whitey, and I drove around the countryside, looking for Golden Star. We called and called and used the recorder. We asked neighbors if they had seen our beloved cat. No one had. We looked and searched for ten days, but we couldn't find him.

I fought back the tears that gathered in my eyes. A sinking anguish knotted my stomach. Glenn's face looked bleak with sorrow. He would leave the house, shove his hands in his pockets, hunch his shoulders forward, walk, and look over the fields.

Glenn and I reminisced about Golden Star. We had taken him for rides in our station wagon since he was a kitten. When he became older, he and Whitey would race to the wagon when they knew we were going somewhere.

Many times, Golden Star would get carsick if we traveled a distance, so I carried plenty of paper towels and wipes in the car. If he got sick, I would lay him next to Whitey, who would begin licking him. Whitey's massaging seemed to help the cat recover.

Golden Star had always hunted in the nearby meadow. If he caught a mole, a mouse, or a rat, he would bring it to the porch, place it outside the French doors, and meow for my attention.

Glenn's birthday was August 20, and I began planning a get-together for him. "No!" Glenn protested. "I don't want to see anyone."

His sharp disapproval told me that he was still grieving over Golden Star. I stopped all social preparations, as I didn't want to force myself to look happy. I was grieving too.

Early on the morning of Glenn's birthday, a loud pitiable cry jolted us awake. We jumped out of bed, and I turned on the porch light. We could hear wailing just outside the door. We saw a thin, malnourished, burr-covered, hollow-sided, grimy form—what appeared to be a cat. A bloody paw pressed against the glass; pleading eyes looked at us.

"Golden Star!" Glenn yelled as he jerked open the door and swooped up the matted fur ball. "Golden Star, you've come home for my birthday!"

After patting Golden Star's head, I ran to the kitchen, warmed a bowl of milk, and brought it to him. When Glenn put him down, Golden Star limped to the bowl, dragging a piece of cord tied around his neck.

It seemed as if Golden Star had been a prisoner.

Someone must have stolen him from our home and tied him somewhere. But our cat had gnawed through the cord and struck out for home. We never knew how long or how far he had traveled to get to us. We could only thank God for bringing him home.

After Golden Star's tummy was filled with milk, he and Glenn began celebrating the day together. Glenn brushed, bathed, and towel-dried the cat until we saw the snow-white and golden-yellow fur. "This is the happiest birthday I've ever had," Glenn said.

Today, as I write this story, who do you think is curled up on my lap? Golden Star. Yes, he has us under his paw and we love it.

My Teacher,

My Pet

And Then, Along Came Toby

Lois Allen Skaggs

We had a problem at our house that seemed almost hopeless. Cleo, my husband, had suffered two severe heart attacks and now, unable to work, he had taken to drinking. It was a familiar cycle: a period of sobriety, then a drinking bout, followed by remorse and another stretch of sobriety. Sometimes in those drying-out periods, I'd find him sitting on the edge of our bed, staring at the floor. The humiliation in his face—his sad brown eyes—would speak for him. "I hate myself. Just look what I'm doing to myself. I should be taking care of you."

Many times I'd think I couldn't go through it again. I'd cry out to God, "Oh, help this man who is so unhappy with himself. Help me; I don't know what to do. Please, please, take over."

And then, along came Toby—a kitten. My daughter Ann was in the process of moving to her own apartment, and Toby started out as her pet. "Mom," she said one day, "I bought a little Siamese cat. Can I bring him here till I move? Just for a few weeks?"

Inwardly I groaned. To me, pet was spelled p-e-s-t.

But what could I say? Ann had already bought him. "Okay," I said reluctantly. "But only till you move."

"Thanks, Mom." She grinned. "Oh, you'll love him; wait and see."

"I doubt that." But, as I discovered, Toby was hard to dislike.

He had limpid blue eyes and tiny eyelashes. His fawn-colored coat was soft and shiny—long for a Siamese; his ears, paws, and "mask" were a deep, dark chocolate brown. He was the "washingest" kitty I'd ever seen. Lying in the sun on our back porch, he'd lick one little brown paw with his tongue and scrub his ear again and again, then do the other one.

I'd always heard that Siamese were likely to be aloof. Not this one. He actually seemed to pursue us and seek affection. Especially from Cleo.

Shortly before her moving day, Ann got some bad news. "I can't take Toby with me, Mom. The landlord says 'no pets.' I guess I'll see if my friend Tammy can take him to her family's farm."

Cleo and I talked it over. When Ann moved, Toby stayed.

We let him come and go as he wanted. Soon I could open the back screen door, yell "Toby!" and he'd come running as fast as he could, his paws barely touching the ground. He ran after birds, butterflies. On his first excursion up our walnut tree, he got stuck. When it began to rain, we had to ask our neighbor Ron, who owns a tall ladder, to rescue him.

Before long, Toby established routines with Cleo and me. In the morning, he'd hop up on our bed, settle down between us, and purr us awake. When I came home from my job as a switchboard operator on the evening shift at Farmington Community Hospital, Toby met me at the back door—as if to remind me that he'd been doing his job of keeping Cleo company while I was gone. It was a job he took very seriously.

He played with Cleo constantly; and when Cleo took a nap, Toby curled up at the foot of the bed to take a nap too. If Cleo watched television, Toby climbed into his lap. He followed Cleo everywhere. When Cleo worked in the yard, Toby had to inspect everything that was done. Cleo even asked his opinion.

"How's that, boy? Think that will do?"

Silence.

"Yeah, I think so too."

When Cleo walked across the driveway to sit with Ron on his porch steps for a neighborly chat, Toby would follow and lie between his feet, patiently waiting. After the visit, Cleo would say, "Well, Toby, let's be on our way," and off they'd go, Toby trailing behind.

Watching, smiling to myself, I'd think, *I do believe that cat thinks he's a dog.*

One evening Cleo was sitting in his favorite chair, a recliner, leaning back with his hands clasped behind his head. Toby jumped onto the table by the chair and meowed, looking intently at Cleo.

"What do you want, Toby?" Cleo said.

"Meow."

"What do you want, boy?"

"Meow, meow," Toby cried, louder.

Taking his hands down, Cleo leaned forward. "Toby, I don't know what you want!"

Toby promptly sprang up and stretched out full-length along the top of the backrest—his favorite spot on Cleo's favorite chair.

When he told me about it later, Cleo said, "That boy can talk. He was telling me to move my arms out of the way."

Toby was telling Cleo something else too. Something we didn't recognize till later.

After breakfast one morning, Toby went to the back door, meowed, and sat down. That meant he wanted out. Cleo opened the door, but Toby just sat still and looked up at him.

"Well, go on out, if you want, boy." Cleo nudged him lightly, so out he went.

An hour or so later, someone knocked at the front door. Cleo went to answer it. I heard a man's voice ask, "Do you own a Siamese cat?"

"Yes, we do," Cleo replied.

"You'd better come with me," the man said.

I dropped to my knees. "Oh, no, Lord. Please, no!"

Cleo came in through the back door. His chin was trembling so much that he could hardly get the words out. "Toby's been hit! Honey, he's dead."

"Oh, Cleo!"

"He's lying on the back porch. The man said that he just

couldn't help it. Toby jumped in front of the truck. He wasn't mangled; he looks like he's sleeping."

Cleo choked out the next words. "He loved me!"

"I know, honey."

"He loved me just the way I am."

"I know."

For a while, we didn't speak. Then I put my arms around him. "You know, Cleo, that's the way God loves you too. Just like you are. His love is just like Toby's, only more intense. His love follows you too."

We stood silently, holding each other, for a minute. Then Cleo went down to the basement and found an old tin breadbox and some soft cloth to line it. He took it out to the back porch. I stayed inside. I didn't want to see Toby. I wanted to remember him alive.

From the window, I watched Cleo carry the box and a shovel down to the back of the garden where he and Toby had spent so much time together. He dug a tiny grave under the peach tree.

I bowed my head. "Lord, is it wrong to love a cat that much?"

The answer came gently, firmly into my mind: *Through that cat, your husband has been able to feel my love. I sent Toby.*

"Oh, yes, Lord. Thank you."

I peeped out the window again. Cleo was just sitting on the ground, holding the shovel, his head bowed. He sat there a long time, telling Toby goodbye. From that time on the binges stopped. Cleo began going to church with me. No more than a month later—just before Christmas—he committed his life to Christ. As for me, I'm still learning every day that God's ways are "past finding out." He loves us so generously, so forgivingly. He can even use a little cat to show us that.

Bed of Roses

Marion Bond West

I was overjoyed when my husband, Gene, surprised me with a beautiful Persian area rug.

For years I had admired them and wished that one day I could own one. The rug was perfect in front of our fireplace, and it picked up the dark green, beige, and rose colors of our living room. As we stood admiring it, our cat, Minnie, stepped cautiously onto the plush rug and settled down in the center of a bouquet of pale pink roses.

"No!" I raised my voice. Our dear Minnie was surprised; she had unlimited access to every square inch of our house, but now I was trying to train her to respect this one bit of space.

That night I got up to find Minnie back on the rug, sleeping on the roses once again. I scolded her, and she left reluctantly. Perhaps I was a bit overprotective; but for now, while the rug was brand-new, I didn't want to risk it getting soiled.

Then, very early one morning, I came downstairs and discovered that Minnie had positioned herself so that the tips of her front paws barely touched the fringe of the rug; the rest of her body was safely not touching it at all! She looked at me very innocently and pitifully, purring as if to say, "Surely you can't object to this!"

Well, I finally felt a little silly. Minnie just wanted a soft, comfortable spot to nap, and she seemed to enjoy lying on those pink roses. After all, this wasn't a museum, but a living room, a room to live in. How could I turn away anyone, human or animal, seeking safety and warmth?

"It's okay, girl," I assured Minnie. She purred with her eyes closed, and her paws barely touched the fringe of the new rug she so loved. I went back to bed happily and drifted off to sleep thinking, *In any contest of wills between humans and felines, I know who usually wins.* Sleep came quickly.

We all seek the comfort of God's sheltering arms. My own "bed of roses" is in the warm safety of his love.

The Angel Cat

Susan Chernak McElroy

During the first months following my cancer diagnosis, I wouldn't acknowledge any kind of healing but physical healing. I wasn't interested in techniques that could help me cope better or extend my life expectancy by a few months; the possibility of remission or improving my quality of life didn't capture my attention either. Full recovery was the only option I would accept, and I was willing to do anything and go anywhere to achieve it.

When my surgeries and radiation treatments were over, I found myself in that frightening twilight zone of life after treatment. The doctors had done all they could, and I was on my own to wonder if I'd be alive or dead by the following year.

For the sake of my sanity, I tried hard to convince myself and anyone else who would listen that I was doing just fine and that cancer was no death sentence. My motto became, "I don't write off cancer patients." I was ferocious and flailing.

Only two weeks earlier, my partner and I had parted ways. I was feeling confused and frightened about the future. Alone in bed at night, I would look at the white walls and wonder who would want a thirty-nine-year-old cancer patient. Life in my apartment was dismally quiet.

Then Flora entered my life—a skinny feral kitten about four weeks old, full of ringworm, fleas, and ear mites. Shivering and alone under the wheel well of my parked car, Flora looked desperately sick. I grabbed ahold of her scraggly tail and tugged. Within seconds my hand was scratched to shreds, but I hung on and brought her, hissing and complaining, to my apartment. At that point, I realized that my lonely life welcomed the commotion of a tiny, angry kitten who would distract me from my own depressing thoughts.

With the arrival of the kitten, I pulled my energy away from myself and my fretful imaginings and concentrated on healing Flora. Along with ringworm and fleas, she had a terrible viral infection that had ulcerated her tongue, cheeks, and throat. I knew all about ulcers in the mouth, so I sympathized wholeheartedly with her miserable condition. It took weeks, but slowly Flora healed, and along the way we bonded. Soon, she was a loving, trusting ball of black-and-white fuzz who met me at my door each evening when I returned from work. The loneliness of my apartment vanished, and I cherished the success of our health venture together. Although my own future looked uncertain, success with Flora seemed to be something I could achieve.

Only weeks after I'd finally nursed Flora back to some resemblance of healthy kittenhood, she was diagnosed with feline leukemia.

Cancer.

Her veterinarian gave her the same sorry prognosis my oncologist had given me: Flora would most likely die within a year or two.

My response was instant and unconscious. As soon as Flora's vet handed down the diagnosis, I wrote her off as a lost cause. Quickly, my emotional attachment to her ceased as I began to protect myself from the pain of her death, which I knew would come. The veterinarian had told me Flora would die, and I simply accepted this; I stopped speaking to Flora and playing with her, because when I did I would end up sobbing hysterically for my kitten. It became difficult for me to even look at her.

But Flora simply wouldn't let me pull away. When I'd walk past her, she'd chase after me. Her paw touched my cheek hesitantly each night as she curled up next to me in bed, her purr resonant and strong. If my mood was chilly, she seemed not to notice. Flora did what cats do best—she waited and watched.

Her patience finally won out. One night I had an *Aha!* experience about my attitude toward Flora. How could I believe that my own cancer wasn't a death sentence when I couldn't see the same hope for her? How could I dismiss any being without dismissing myself? Although I was busy blathering about hope and healing, I knew that I honestly saw myself in the grave.

That realization was a profound turning point for me. It was slow in coming, but when it did, it hit me like a downpour of hailstones. How often in my life had I turned away from pain and loss, and from honest feelings? Living a half-life, I'd put away emotion at the first inkling of loss and had nearly lost myself in the process.

One night shortly after my awakening, I lit a candle for Flora and myself. We sat together looking at the flame, and I vowed to Flora that I would love her with wild abandon for as long as she was with me, because loving her felt so good. Pulling away from her hurt, and I didn't need any more painful isolation in my life. In loving Flora, I knew I would find a way to love myself as well—poor diagnosis and all. For both of us, each day of life would be a day we could celebrate together.

I began a quest to heal Flora that included many of the same gems of complementary medicine I was attempting on myself. Flora got acupressure; vitamins; homeopathy; music and color therapies; detoxifying baths; and unlimited quantities of hugs, love, and affection. Her water bowl had tiny, colorful crystals in it. Her collar was a healing green.

What was most important in this process, though, was the attitude change I experienced from this mumbo jumbo, as some of my bewildered friends called it. Healing stopped being so painfully heavy. It became fun, even silly. When I told my friends I might have my house visited by dowsers to seek out and correct "bad energy vibrations," I darn well had to have a highly developed sense of humor.

Over the next few months, I slowly learned that healing is more than heroics over illness. Healing isn't simply an end result, it's a process. Flora helped me reclaim the joy that had died after my cancer treatment and my previous relationship had ended. She brought me tremendous peace with her quiet, trusting presence. Finally, as I saw Flora healed, loved, and cherished, I knew I could honestly hold the same hopeful vision for myself.

Flora is sleek, happy, and seven years old today. Her last three tests for leukemia have been negative. At the time of my *Aha!* with Flora, I felt that she was an angel sent to teach me that turning away from love accomplishes nothing. I believe that Flora was ready to die to bring me her message . . . if it would have taken that.

LA Blues

Lisa Huntress

I was thrilled when my husband, Scott, announced he'd been transferred and we'd be moving from Kansas City to Los Angeles. I saw LA as an exciting city, full of fascinating if somewhat intimidating people. We found an apartment on the beach with a view of the ocean. While my husband put in long hours at his new job, I explored the area, looking forward to meeting my new neighbors.

I hardly had a chance. People flew by on Rollerblades and listened to music on headsets instead of stopping to chat. It certainly wasn't the slow, friendly pace of Kansas City I was used to. The sun looked like a pale orange disk through the pollution, and cars clogged the freeways. I got a marketing job at one of the movie studios, but my coworkers seemed more interested in their careers than being friends with me.

Disillusionment settled over me like, well, the smog. Scott had to travel on business for long stretches at a time, and increasingly I found myself all alone in Los Angeles. After work I went straight home. *Why try to make friends with these people?* I figured.

One Saturday as I was heading out on an errand, I saw a group of children huddled by the oleanders outside our building.

Peering out between the thick, leathery leaves was a striped gray cat. "Here, kitty, kitty," one little girl said as she knelt and reached out her hand.

"Don't get too close!" a neighbor yelled from his deck. "He's nasty. He'll bite." Sure enough, the cat hissed and lashed out, sending the children scurrying.

I looked reproachfully at the man who had yelled. "That cat is wild," he informed me. "He's been living in those bushes, eating scraps and whatever else."

Well, I knew cats. And I knew that cats generally gave as good as they got. A few days later I heard two kids tease him as they braked their bikes on the sandy sidewalk. "Hey, Bruno!" they taunted and got a hiss from him. *So he has a name.* The next time I walked by his bush, I called, "Bruno, Bruno."

He replied with his trademark hiss. He probably feels out of place too, I decided. My own defenses went up later when I heard one of the neighbors shout, "I'm going to kill that cat!" I had to help Bruno. He needed a home and he needed it now.

The one thing Bruno understood was food. I bought some kitty tuna, put it on our deck in a bowl, and caught him nibbling furtively. The next day he was back again, gobbling what I'd put out, but darting off when I got too close. Each day I moved the dish closer to our door, as I talked quietly to him. One day I reached out and gave him a scratch behind his ears. He arched his back and hissed, then went back to eating. At least he didn't run off.

A week or two later, when I moved the dish onto our

living room floor, Bruno cautiously ventured inside to get his dinner. I kept talking as I pulled the front door shut, then I sat on the floor. "Welcome to your new home, Bruno," I announced.

To my surprise, he took to life indoors right away, even though he made himself scarce. As soon as I came home from work, he would scamper under the bed. It was a little like living with a phantom cat. I put out food in the living room, then watched from around the corner as he ate it up.

After about three months, Bruno began to come out of his shell. If I sat very still he let me stroke his back without trying to bite me. "You'll be okay here," I assured him one evening. "Nobody will hurt you." At the same time I began to resent the neighbors even more. Why hadn't they helped him? Why hadn't people showed they cared? Typical.

One night Bruno wouldn't eat. The next night, the same thing. What was wrong? Before long, his eyes and the skin beneath his fur started looking yellow. *Maybe he needs some vitamins.* I mixed some into his food. He wouldn't touch it. I didn't relish the thought of taking him to the vet, but clearly it was time. I got a pet carrier and lured Bruno inside with some catnip, then took him off to an animal clinic. "We'll keep him for the night," said the woman at the desk, "so we can run some tests."

The veterinarian called me the next day. "Bruno has fatty liver disease," he said. "He's not able to absorb nutrients from his food. The humane thing to do is euthanize him."

"I have to think about this," I said. I got Bruno and

brought him back to the apartment. When I let him out of the carrier, he actually curled up in my lap and purred. He was glad to be home.

"Please, God," I prayed, "don't let Bruno die." Scott was on business in China, but I called him there and asked him to pray for Bruno too. By the time I hung up, I was practically in tears. I'd had to telephone halfway around the world to find a caring voice.

The next day I got a call at work. "Hi, Lisa," a man said, "I'm a colleague of Scott's in the LA office. When he checked in this morning, he told me about your cat. I have a suggestion."

Someone in Los Angeles actually cared? "There's a great holistic clinic not far from you," he continued. "They do acupuncture there. Why don't you try it?"

I explained that Bruno would hardly let anyone touch him, much less poke him with needles. "But I really appreciate your calling," I said. "It was nice of you."

The call made me realize I needed to get a second opinion on Bruno. I found another vet who came up with the same diagnosis—but a different plan of action. "No, you don't need to put him to sleep," he said. "He's not suffering. There's still hope."

The doctor inserted a tube in Bruno's neck so I could feed and medicate him at home. Every day after work I spent hours feeding Bruno through his tube. I had to help him. He was the only friend I had.

After Scott returned from China he pitched in, but

nonetheless the stress was taking its toll on me. One morning a colleague said, "You okay, Lisa? You look tired." I started telling him about Bruno. People stopped by my cubicle to listen. Soon they were offering advice and sharing their own pet traumas. The next day a blond I'd once dismissed as being straight out of *Baywatch* brought me some catnip. "I'll put Bruno in my prayers too," she promised.

One night Bruno grew so weak I rushed him to an animal hospital emergency room at three o'clock in the morning. Even in the middle of the night the waiting room was filled with cats, rabbits, birds, dogs, reptiles, and their owners. A German shepherd limped over to inspect Bruno, but Bruno couldn't muster a hiss. "What are you here for?" the dog's owner asked, and we had one of those heart-to-heart talks about the ailments of our pets.

I noticed the other people in the waiting room nodding their heads in understanding. They looked just like the people I saw rushing by on the sidewalk and zooming past my car on the freeway. Had I really given LA a chance on its own terms? Had I been the one in too much of a hurry—a hurry to judge my new neighbors?

The vet treated Bruno with an IV and then sent us home. Gradually Bruno started to gain weight, and bit by bit he regained his old swagger. But he was a different Bruno. Less fearful, kinder, a little more willing to trust. Now when the vet and the workers in the clinic put out a hand to pet him, Bruno actually allowed a caress and purred.

The day the vet removed his feeding tube was a cause for

great celebration. My new friends at work sent home a huge canister of fancy gourmet cat snacks for him. That afternoon I held Bruno in my arms on our apartment steps and we sat there looking at the ocean. The warm sun poured through the palm trees as Rollerbladers streaked past, and every once in a while someone would stop to admire my cat.

"May I pet him?" one little boy asked.

"Not yet," I said. "He's still getting used to strangers. But he's getting better."

And so was I.

The Last One
to Leave

Jeanne Hill

Our cozy little ranch house in a pleasant Scottsdale, Arizona, subdivision was now hugely silent. Dixon, our youngest of three, had been packed off to college, and my husband, Louis, had just departed for an evening community meeting. I was knee-deep in castoff teenage belongings in Dixon's closet, trying to clean it out, when Kiff, Dixon's silver tabby, appeared. She meowed forlornly. She was a kind of castoff too, now that Dixon was gone. She had been a gift to Dixon when she was eight weeks old and he a kindergartner.

"Oh, Kiff," I sighed, "don't carry on so. I miss him too!" I had never thought this would happen to me. When our children—first David and then Dawn—had left, I welcomed my new freedom. And after all, with a vigorous family of five, we really had been shoehorned into our little house. But I hadn't anticipated the silence and, well . . . the emptiness, in both the house and me now that all the children were gone.

Louis had a very busy schedule as a professor of engineering at Arizona State, and Kiff was hardly what you'd call company, especially now that she was moping around all day. She and Dixon had been buddies. At night Kiff always slept at the foot of Dixon's bed. During the day I could always spot Dixon from my kitchen window by Kiff's pluming tail, which was an elegant, furry flag of silver-gray.

Now she watched sulkily as I packed away a green papier-mâché remnant of "the grand volcano," Dixon's elaborate seventh-grade science project. He and a friend, Frank, had worked for days on a "spectacular" demonstration of a volcanic eruption. They'd buried red food coloring and Alka-Seltzer tablets in the volcano's pit, which they planned to activate by pumping fluid through plastic tubing hidden in the hall. On the first trial run, I was posted at the volcano table in Dixon's room to observe the fiery eruption. The boys pumped mightily from the hall, but nothing happened. Dixon thought for sure that they'd failed—until Frank spotted Kiff planted firmly on the plastic tubing under the table.

Even in high school Dixon had managed an afterschool snack with us and a romp with Kiff before he hurried off to chess club, Scouts, or play practice. He often brought home a small pizza then to share with Kiff and me. So I'd bought one yesterday—but it didn't taste the same, somehow.

At three-thirty every day since Dixon left, Kiff had positioned herself on the windowsill, watching for Dixon's old green Chevy to chug into the driveway. When he didn't show up, after a while a low moaning cry would start deep in her throat and eventually turn into a loud, mournful lament. In truth, I felt like moaning myself.

"Face it, Kiff," I said, stroking her back comfortingly. "You're a leftover cat from Dixon's childhood, just as I'm a leftover mom."

When Louis came home and we prepared for bed, he went into Dixon's room and carried Kiff into ours, laying her gently on the fleecy comforter at our feet.

By the next evening I'd finally finished my job of packing Dixon's keepsakes into the storeroom. I was tired; so was Louis. He'd had a busy day. We sat down to dinner and had no sooner touched our first bites when Kiff startled us with her mournful howling from Dixon's room. "You and that cat!" Louis said irritably. "For my sake, I wish you'd both adjust to Dixon's leaving! That cat bawls all night, so I can't sleep, and you've even quit cooking. I didn't leave home, you know. Only the kids left."

I flinched. "That's not fair!" I snapped.

"No? Just take a good look at dinner tonight—warmed-up, leftover, dried-out pizza!"

He had a point there; I'd done a lot better at "family" meals than the orangish lumps now on our plates.

"And look at yourself!" Louis's voice was quieter now but still irritable. "Do you realize you're wearing Dawn's old slacks, David's discarded shirt—and Dixon's Scout neckerchief knotted around your hair? I mean, this isn't like you, and it's been going on for three weeks now."

"I didn't realize," I said, looking down at the strange ensemble I'd come across yesterday in the storeroom and absently donned today. Until that moment I really hadn't realized how lonely I'd been. "Sorry, honey," I said, "I'll try to clean up my act."

But in the morning my loneliness was just as acute when I opened the Bible for our daily breakfast devotional. How I longed to hear Dixon's strong young voice reading! But this morning mine would have to suffice because Louis had read yesterday. I turned to our place marked in 2 Corinthians (5:17), where we'd left off yesterday . . . and I couldn't believe the verse! "Therefore, if any one is in Christ, he is a new creation," I read. "The old has passed away, behold, the new has come" (RSV). That last part struck a new and different chord with me, even as I went on reading.

After Louis kissed me and went to work, I reread that verse: ". . . the old has passed away, behold, the new . . ." Could God be trying to tell me something? The old was my kids' childhoods, I felt, but what new could there be for an old, leftover mom? With my storeroom work done now and no excuse to linger in Dixon's room, I felt the day hanging heavy on my hands.

Kiff wandered aimlessly in and out of the door until shortly after lunch. Then she was gone all afternoon. She didn't even show up at three-thirty—Dixon's old snack time. By four I was concerned. Might she have left the safety of our side street for the more heavily traveled one next to us? She would get run over; she was getting older and less agile. I'd check.

I put on a jacket and walked halfway down the block before I saw Kiff's pluming tail in the midst of three little girls from the neighborhood! While I watched, unnoticed, one of the dark-haired girls pulled a doll's yellow bonnet around Kiff's head and tied it under her chin. To my amazement (Kiff never liked anything over her ears), Dixon's tabby stood perfectly still. *Way to go, Kiff!* I thought. *You've found your "new." Now, if only I could.*

I'd no more than turned back toward the house when what that old cat had done hit home with me. I'd never find my "new" unless I went looking for it the way Kiff had.

But where to look? I pondered that, moments later, standing at the kitchen stove. Maybe I'd start my "new" with a special dinner for Louis. Why not fix something I wouldn't cook if Dixon were home? Hmmm . . . Dixon's least-favorite food was steak. So we'd splurge tonight and have steak—by candlelight! (Dixon always complained about candlelight: "I can't see what I'm eating, Mom. How about if I turn on the lights?")

That night no one turned on the lights nor complained about the "forties music." We enjoyed a first in many years—a romantic dinner with flickering candles and sweet music.

After dinner Louis mentioned his friend at work, Dick Raymond. "Dick's mother is in that rest home near us. He says that some of the people there don't get many visitors. I was thinking that, if you were to stop over . . ." Louis closed his hand over mine, ". . . maybe you could cure two cases of loneliness—theirs and yours."

The next day, somewhat hesitantly, I visited with three people in that rest home. The following week my list grew to five. Soon I had a regular group I read to, and I began to look forward to my visits. I also began to feel better about myself. Like Kiff, I had found a new circle of friends— and a new sense of purpose and usefulness. The emptiness at home suddenly turned into serenity. For the first time in years, I had time for chatty letters to distant friends, long (and uninterrupted!) soaks in the tub, and leisurely suppers with Louis. I even enrolled in an Old Testament course at a nearby community college.

And so it goes. In time Louis got an exciting new appointment as dean of engineering at the University of Akron, and we picked up and moved with the ease of newly-weds. The passage in Corinthians that I chanced upon is still working. Indeed, I will always try to let go of the old and seek the new. By the way, it's a lesson Kiff hasn't forgotten either. When we left for Akron, our son David moved into our Scottsdale house, and Kiff stayed with him. Just the other day he told me that he caught a glimpse of her sidling up to a high school student down the block!

Purring and Praising

Marion Bond West

J erry had taken a Friday off from work and we were eating breakfast at the local Waffle House, a couple of miles from our home. It was a rare treat—just the two of us. And I love eating breakfast out. As we got up to leave, I noticed through the window two young men bending down outside. I couldn't see what they were bending toward, but in my heart I *knew* it was a cat! It hadn't been outside when we entered, so someone had probably dumped it while we ate.

Maybe the men will take it, I hoped. *Oh, Lord, let them take the cat. Please don't let me have to walk by an abandoned kitten.* I saw the men get into their car. Neither of them held a kitten.

"Jerry," I whispered as we stood at the cash register, "I believe there's a stray cat outside."

A look of agony crossed his face. Not for the cat, but for the fact that we had to walk by it. He knew my weakness. I reminded him, "I've been doing pretty good lately. I'm getting to where I can walk right by stray cats, even if they look me in the eye."

Jerry sighed and his jaw flinched slightly.

We went outside; and there stood the small kitten—skinny, dirty, tired, and quite obviously abandoned. His face and ears had black dirt caked on them. He'd somehow stepped into tar and it had dried on his paws.

As we went outside, the aroma of bacon escaped with us. The red kitten was young and pitifully thin. A few feet away, cars whizzed by on the expressway. He wouldn't last long. Nevertheless, I got ready to walk by him—I wasn't even going to pet him or say "Hi, kitty," or go back in and get him a piece of bacon.

But then the foolish cat, with everything in the world against him, did the most amazing thing. He rubbed up against my leg and purred, long and loud.

Purred! Half-starved, filthy, no hope of getting any of the bacon from the Waffle House, people ignoring him, and the stupid cat purred just like he was clean, well fed, and loved.

Without hesitation I stooped and picked him up and held him close. I could see the fleas on him. He looked right into my eyes and purred some more. Then he laid his head on my shoulder for a moment. I could feel his heart pounding. Even in fear, he purred.

If he'd meowed loudly, scampered under a bush, or just sat silently by the door, I could have walked by him. Jerry and I continued toward the car without speaking. Jerry looked grimly ahead. I held the purring kitten and smiled foolishly. "I'll try to find him a home," I said, without looking at my husband.

"Who in the world would take that ugly cat?"

"He has a beautiful face—underneath the dirt." Jerry had planned to stop at the bank; and when he did, I got out and went inside with him. I went to each teller's window and asked, "Would you like a kitten?" No one even smiled at me. The cat purred in my arms.

Jerry glared at me from across the bank lobby as if to say, "I'm not impressed by your attempts."

At home I fed the cat and Jerry asked, "Is it a female?"

"I don't know. Don't think so."

"You never do."

I bathed the cat and fed him some more. Then he hopped into a little basket I'd placed in the kitchen for him, gave a big sigh, and went to sleep on his back with his paws crooked slightly up in the air.

The vet assured me our new kitten was a male, and I promptly named him Joshua. I'd had this strong wall built around my heart that didn't permit any more cats inside. Then Joshua's purring had made the wall come tumbling down, just like the biblical Joshua's marching had caused the walls of Jericho to collapse.

By Joshua's sixth day with us, I'd catch Jerry bending over to pet him. Sometimes he'd say softly, "Hi, cat. You're looking better." Joshua picked the foot of our bed to sleep on at night, after he became certain it was safe. He'd lie very still in order to be able to stay.

I continued to marvel that the cat's purring had resulted in his finding a good home with all the comforts of life. Finally, I saw a scriptural parallel one day when I was telling someone that we should remember to praise the Lord in all situations—even bad ones. I had said, "Anyone can praise the Lord when things are going great, but how it must please and honor God when we make a joyful noise in the midst of gloom and despair."

Right then I wondered if God doesn't feel a little like I had when that desperately hungry and abandoned cat looked up at me and purred, seeming to expect only the best. Why, I'd been overwhelmed. I simply had to respond to his "faith" in me.

Everyone knows that starving cats shouldn't purr. They should meow frantically and complain loudly.

Purring and praising seem to be a lot alike, I've decided. Sometimes now when I feel like complaining, giving up, or bellowing noisily, I remember skinny, hungry Joshua and how he purred his heart out that day at the Waffle House. Remembering helps me realize the importance of praising God, especially in bad situations.

It doesn't seem logical that I could see such a powerful truth simply by picking up a stray cat, but then nothing gets my attention as quickly as a stray cat; and the Lord knows that. So, like Joshua, who just leaned up against me and purred away, I want to learn to lean against my Father and praise away, regardless of my circumstances.

Three Little Kittens

Phyllis Hobe

In my rural area I often see barn cats hunting in the fields. In exchange for keeping the rodent population down, they get food and shelter from farmers, but they aren't comfortable with people. If they wander onto my property, they run off as soon as they see me.

One morning, however, I found a cat curled up beneath the shrubs in front of my house. It was pregnant, a pretty little gray cat with black stripes. I brought out some food, which the cat gobbled up. She let me pet her and rubbed against me, purring. This was no barn cat. It was a family pet.

I called everyone in my neighborhood, but no one reported a missing cat. I tried the local police, the animal shelter, several veterinarians—with no success. It seemed probable that she had been abandoned by her owners. It also was obvious that she was going to deliver her kittens very soon.

What was I to do? I couldn't bring her into my home because she might be diseased. But it was October, and though the days were warm, the nights were cold. At sunset she let me pick her up and I took her into my garage. She curled up on a pile of old towels and at that moment she went into labor.

127

For the next few hours, I watched in awe as the cat delivered three kittens. From what I could see, they were not only alive, but vigorous. "As soon as you can, start picking them up and petting them," my veterinarian said when I called him. "That way, when you want to find homes for them, they'll be ready to live with people."

Find homes for three kittens? I hadn't thought of that. I called the animal shelter, but I was told that if I brought them in they would have to be put to sleep immediately. "It's the way it is," the woman told me. "The newborns and mother might have diseases our other animals could catch." There was a sadness in her voice. "If you can keep them for six weeks, when they finish nursing we can take them in."

Six weeks, I thought. *But maybe I can find them homes before that.*

My house isn't large, and I already had two cats and one dog, so I carried the mother and her kittens down to the basement and piled newspapers and old towels in a box for a nesting place. Of course, my other animals were curious, and it took some athletic maneuvering to get past them every time I used the basement door.

"Lord, I've got six weeks," I prayed. "I need all the help you can give me." I called everyone I knew and passed the word. I ran an ad in the local paper. I even told people I didn't know well and asked them to tell their friends. I kept getting turned down. It seemed that people who loved cats already had one or more. *Surely,* I told myself, *someone will come forward.*

No one did. As the weeks passed I felt uneasy. Was God

going to abandon the animals just the way some human had? I couldn't believe that. But the kittens—two females and a male—were getting bigger, learning how to jump and climb; and I couldn't keep them in the basement much longer. My veterinarian examined them and gave them rabies shots, so I knew they were healthy.

But when I called the animal shelter they had bad news for me. They were overwhelmed with kittens; they couldn't promise to keep them for long. *I can't let them be put to sleep.*

On the last day of the sixth week, I reminded God that we had come to our deadline yet nothing was happening. And then it hit me: I had given God an ultimatum. I had more or less told him I would have faith in him for six weeks and no more.

I was so ashamed. "Forgive me, Lord," I prayed. "I know you will help me find homes for these little ones. However long it takes, I'll look after them."

A sense of peace came over me. For the first time, I allowed the kittens and their mother to follow me upstairs. I trusted my very friendly dog and cats to accept them; and after a bit of curious sniffing, they did.

When the kittens were eight weeks old, a friend of a friend called and asked if she could see them. When she did, she fell in love with them and took one of the females home with her. Two days later I had a call from a young couple whose cat had died a month earlier. "We miss him so much," the woman said. They took the rambunctious young male with them. By the next week the third kitten went home with the young man who delivers my fuel oil.

That left the mother cat, whom I decided to keep. Like my animals, she wasn't young and spent most of her time sleeping. But then I had a call from a friend's neighbor. "I'm getting on in years and so is my cat," the woman told me. "We need some company, but neither of us can keep up with a kitten. I was wondering if you would let me have the mother."

These events happened three years ago, and all four cats are doing well. As for me, I learned a valuable lesson. Now, when I need God's help, I simply ask, knowing he will come to my aid. And I don't give him a deadline.

Q: Is There a God?
A: Meow!

Mary Ellen "Angel Scribe"

At twenty-five years of age, I began exploring spirituality. I knew there was a God, but I couldn't see or feel God. You might have called me a believing skeptic.

Around that time, my husband, Howard, and I took our first vacation together. We rented a motor home and brought along our shaded-silver Persian cats, Channel and Camelot. We left Vancouver Island, Canada, and headed to Lake Chelan in Washington State. At the campsite, we put the cats on their harness-leashes. A short time later, we noticed that Camelot had wiggled free of his harness and was gone.

Of all the animal companions I've loved, this shy, gentle creature most relied on me and trusted that I'd protect him. I had adopted Camelot from someone who raised him in a cage, so the cat had not learned how to fend for himself.

We were devastated at the thought of losing Camelot. We walked around the small town of Chelan, calling for him and offering his favorite treat as a reward if he'd return, but to no avail. For the next four days and three nights, we wandered the streets all day and into the wee hours of the morning. We left word of our precious Persian's disappearance at the radio

131

station, newspaper, and local schools, soliciting the help of the townsfolk in the search for our missing cat.

As the sun rose on the last morning of our vacation, we were still walking around the town calling out for Camelot. Since it was four in the morning and we had to return home, we knew this was our last chance to find him. We had done everything humanly possible, and I recognized that Camelot's fate was out of my hands. At that point, I passed my heart into the hands of God and said, "If you are really out there, if you really exist, please show me where my cat is."

The most unusual thing happened next. I felt the invisible hands of God—or perhaps the hands of loving angels—on my back. These hands guided me in the opposite direction from where we'd been walking. They then pressured me to turn to the right, walk another block, and walk to the end of the street. I followed their guidance for about a quarter mile, and then the feeling lifted. I felt confused. "What was that all about?" I wondered.

I called "Camelot" one last time. From under a bush, twenty feet in front of me, a scared, thinner, fluffy, silver Persian cat meowed. Camelot walked out and stood there, waiting for me to pick him up. He blinked his huge green eyes at me. My heart melted and rejoiced at the same instant.

We carried Camelot back to the trailer and put him in front of the water and food dishes. Channel walked over to him and swatted him on the head with her paw. Her look implied, "You sure caused a lot of trouble."

The story of our missing cat soon spread around the

entire town. When we pulled out of the motor-home park for the long trip back to Vancouver Island, we told the gatekeeper that we'd found our cat, and she burst into tears. She said, "Today is my twenty-first birthday, and finding Camelot safe is the best present anyone could give me." There certainly are kind people all over the world.

Camelot's disappearance for those days helped me discover and understand how the divine power of God works in our lives. The cat's disappearance was necessary for my spiritual growth. If he had not taken flight, I would never have been desperate enough to pray for the first time in my life—and then have the hands of God or his angels lead me to Camelot. For me, this was a miracle—an epiphany.

Is there a God? We must all answer this question in our own way and in our own time. And maybe an animal will help reveal the answer.

The Man Who
Hated Cats

Diane M. Ciarloni

I heard my husband's truck come down the driveway and stop behind our house. The truck door slammed. My office door opened. And slammed. I heard him trudge heavily to the top of the stairs. He found me in the kitchen.

"I need some cat food to take to the barn," he said without preamble.

I paused. I didn't want to say something I shouldn't. It was too harsh to say John hated cats, but it was also far too nice to say he liked them. As a matter of fact, there were times when he found it a bit rough merely to tolerate them, but because felines occupied a large space in my heart, he did the best he could to bear with the purring, meowing, rubbing things. You know, rather like the old adage of "Love me, love my cat."

"Cat food?" I queried hesitantly.

"Yeah. Somebody dropped off two kittens. I thought they'd wander on down the road, but they didn't. They stayed."

Almost afraid to ask, I said, "When did they get there?"

He shrugged his shoulders. I could tell he didn't really want me to know how long they'd gone without food.

"Three or four days ago."

I cringed, but said nothing. I just looked at him.

"I still have mice over there, ya' know. That's why I didn't do anything about them. I thought they might make a couple of good barn cats."

I nodded my head in the affirmative. "I'll get your food," I said. "Do you want me to go with you?" I was dying to see them, but John indicated I wasn't needed.

"Not this evening. I'm tired, and you'll spend half the night over there goo-gooing at them. But, just so you'll know something, I'll tell you that one is gray with gray stripes, and the other one looks like a Siamese."

"Do you think they're from the same litter?" I asked.

"I suppose so," he said. "They're exactly the same size. I'll bet there's not a quarter-inch difference in their height. And they stick together like glue. 'Course, I don't understand how two kittens from the same litter can look so different."

He was still shaking his head as I handed him a bag of food. I assumed he was returning to the farm to feed the youngsters rather than waiting until morning. I was right.

I had a very strange feeling about this situation. I thought about it while John was gone. He really did not like cats. At our house, it wasn't at all unusual to hear such pronouncements as:

"Diane, Bubba's looking at my boot really funny. Don't you dare let him go the bathroom in it." Or . . .

"Diane, there's a cat hair in my salad. Oh, Lord, here's a whole glob of cat hair!" Or . . .

"Diane, a cat threw up in the middle of the living-room floor."

It seemed almost constant, which is why I wondered about his posturing over this latest kitty dumping. He should have been irate. He should have said things about taking the kittens to the animal shelter which was less than three miles from the farm. But, instead, he decided to feed them. Something was wrong.

Two days passed before either of us mentioned the kittens again. I was the one who broke the silence.

"How are the kittens?" I asked.

"Fine. They're growing but they're still pretty little."

"I imagine they have fleas like crazy," I said.

He nodded his head in the affirmative. "Yeah, they do."

How did he know, I wondered. Generally speaking, it's impossible to see fleas when looking from any kind of distance. And, given John's chronic myopia, it would be impossible for him to see a flea unless—unless—he'd picked up the tiny bodies and actually inspected them. Surely not. I honestly didn't know how much longer I could stand being caged in this prison of not knowing.

"You know," I said, "just two or three fleas on a tiny body can really make an animal sick. Maybe I should go to the pet supply and hunt for a repellent that's safe for babies. If you intend to keep them, they'll also need their first round of shots. I'll buy the serum and do it myself. Then, when they're older, we'll need to think about spaying and . . ."

Oops. I could tell I may have plunged too far into the kittens' future. I was sure John felt backed into a corner. I immediately began wiggling out of the things I'd said.

"I mean, should you decide to give them away they'll be a lot more appealing to someone if they've been spayed and had their shots."

The statement made sense to John's logical, engineering mind. "Yeah, I s'pose so." We both left it at that.

The next day I bought shots and flea repellents but, rather than going home, I turned in the direction of the farm. The suspense was killing me. I had an urgent, physical need to see these kittens.

"John should be gone," I thought. "He won't be in my way. Besides . . ." My unspoken words trailed off when I spied the tailgate of his truck poking from the leaves of the low tree branches. I pulled quickly to the side of the road, putting the two passenger-side tires nearly in the ditch. I shut off the engine and removed the keys from the ignition in order to silence the alarm.

"Why is he here?" I asked myself as I crept toward the gate. I'd almost reached the drive when I heard voices. I stopped and cocked an ear in that direction. No, I didn't hear voices. Instead, I heard *a* voice. *One* voice. *John's* voice. Why in the world was he talking to himself?

I inched closer, pushing in to the fence and parting the branches. I felt like an idiot, but I had no choice. I cautiously raised up and peered over the branch that was shielding most of my body. I had to slam the palm of my hand over my mouth to prevent myself from blurting out.

John was sitting on one of those molded, white plastic chairs. The gray striped kitten was in his lap, on her back. He was scratching her under the chin and saying ridiculous things in a falsetto voice; things such as "Where did you get that dirt under your chin, little kitty? Have you been in the dirt?" The other kitten, the Siamese-looking one, was draped around the back of his neck. I absolutely could not believe it. I was so shocked that I was basically paralyzed.

I managed to back along the side of the road toward my car. I got in and closed the door just enough to silence the alarm. I wished there was a way for me to get away without starting the engine, but there wasn't. I had to take my chances which, of course, I did. John never heard me. How could he? Every nerve and fiber of his being was too engrossed with those kittens to be aware of anything from the outside world.

It was hard to meet his gaze when he came home that evening.

"Did you get the cat stuff?" he questioned.

I said yes.

"I'm gonna be gone almost all day tomorrow, so why don't you go over there and do whatever you need to do?"

He wasn't fooling me. First, he didn't want to be there because he didn't want those kittens to go running to him in front of me. Second, he didn't want the little buggers to associate anything unpleasant with him.

"Fine," I answered.

Three or four days after I gave them their shots and flea

repellent, John came up the steps carrying a squirming gray kitten.

"Something tried to get them," he explained. "This one was running back and forth across the road in front of the farm. It's a wonder she wasn't run over. I don't know where the other one is. I called for at least forty-five minutes, but she never came."

"How do you know something was after them?" I asked.

"Their food and water were turned over, and this one acts as if she's been badly traumatized. And it's not like the other one not to come when she's called."

I slid my gaze toward him. "You've been calling them a lot?"

Now he started looking downright sheepish. "Well, they had to know when it was time to eat and things like that."

"And what did you call them?"

"I called them kitty and then I used their na——"

He stopped, leaving the end of the word hanging. "Names?" I asked. "They have names?"

"What's wrong with that?" he asked with a hint of belligerence. "Why not have names if they're going to be barn cats?"

"That's fine," I said.

"Puss and Boots," he blurted out.

"What?"

"Puss and Boots," he repeated. "Those are their names. Boots is the gray one with the white feet. Puss is the Siamese—if we ever see her again."

It took all of ten minutes for one thing to become abundantly clear. Boots was *definitely* John's cat. He sat down, and she tore as fast as she could onto his lap. She stood on his chest, put her tiny head about one and one-half inches from his face and cut loose with a very loud meow. I couldn't believe how that kitten's display of affection transformed his usually taciturn visage. It was as if a very, very thick veil dropped away to reveal the pores, fine lines and veins of a real face. It was amazing what a difference it makes when a mask is taken off and put away, even for just a few minutes.

I acted as if I saw nothing strange in his relationship with this kitten. "What do you think about Puss?" I asked.

He shook his head. It was hard to know. We'd been without rain for three months, and were now overrun with coyotes and mountain lions. There'd even been reported sightings of panthers. To hear all that, no one would ever believe we lived less than ten minutes from a major mall; but we were also surrounded by dense woods.

It was two days later when he walked up the stairs carrying a very hungry, very small Siamese kitten. She'd finally come out of hiding, answering his persistent calling.

He was right when he said the kittens stuck together like glue. Puss went running to her rescue if she heard Boots cry and vice versa. They played rough-and-tumble together. They play-fought with one another. They groomed one another like a couple of baby monkeys. But they were also as different as the proverbial day and night.

Boots was spoiled. Period. She wanted John to spend his

time holding her. Not only that, but it was apparent that she felt most deserving of his constant attention. She had a huge meow for such a small body, and she used it constantly to talk to him. Her vocabulary was quite extensive. She had different volume levels and a different pitch for various "words." Her meows changed from one to the other in terms of number of syllables. And she had a habit of sitting up like a squirrel—with perfect balance. It seemed completely natural for her, and she spent a good deal of time in that posture.

And then there was Puss. She was always ever so busy. She had to go here and go there, strutting with great purpose through a room with her tail fixed straight up like a taut mast on a ship. She had practically no meow. It was as if it had been scared out of her whenever she was forced to flee from whatever tried to get her. She sounded like a small, fragile bird making tiny chirps. That was it. She exhibited her own brand of affection and attention, but she was nothing like Boots in that department. For one thing, she absolutely did *not* want to be held. Whenever we tried it, she fought like a mini-tiger. She did, however, like to come up to one of us, press against an ankle and arch her back. We learned she was telling us to scratch her backbone. As we did, she would squirm to her side and then to her back, presenting her vulnerable underside for scratching and gentle patting.

It was difficult to determine who grew the most, John or the kittens. Oh, sure they became physically larger but, in a way, so did he. He seemed to bloom and blossom, with the mask moving back into place less and less frequently. And, gradually, the kittens began growing emotionally but, again, so did he. He learned that a creature whom he once hated (or at least intensely disliked) was able to bring out good and beautiful feelings. Might there not be other creatures—other people—who would do the same? Creatures and people who may have previously been intensely disliked?

Does God not, truly, work in mysterious ways? Is it not truly mysterious how such a powerful Being used two tiny, mewing kittens to transform a very large man who hated cats?

An Inspirational

Friendship

Meet Norton

Peter Gethers

My father absolutely loathed, hated, and despised cats. I tried everything I could think of for his first meeting with Norton. "Don't bring him to the house," he said. I went through my explanation that my guy was different from normal cats, that he was incredibly smart, that he wouldn't bother my father, that at some point in my life, I too thought that I didn't like cats, but when I met Norton that all changed. This had about as much effect on my dad as it would have had on a slab of marble. He was unmoved and simply repeated his instructions: "Don't bring him to the house."

I have to say a few words about my father here. He was as perfect a dad as he could have been. We were terrific pals, and I don't think I could have had more respect for him. For years he was one of the top television writers in LA, and then he became, in his late fifties, one of the top television directors as well. He was a bear of a person, dominating a room with both his looks and his personality. His shtick was to be gruff and cynical, and on the surface he sure was, but in fact he was the most caring and generous man I have ever met in my life. He solved problems and gave advice and was usually just strict enough and unbending enough to provide the right kind of fatherly support. He certainly made plenty of mistakes in his life and his career, but his correct choices more than made up for them. My girlfriend, Cindy—who, for the first two years she knew him, was totally intimidated by him— once said he was the first person she had ever met who was larger than life. I always thought he was funny and smart and talented and exceedingly moral, and I enjoyed being with him and my mother as much as I enjoyed being with my clos- est friends. But he was still my dad and I was still his son— and as such we could, without much provocation, drive each other completely crazy.

As I was taking Norton up to the house for the first time, I had a funny feeling he was going to be another one of those crazy-driving provocations.

The only thing I can really add to the picture, as Norton is about to be introduced to the family, is a brief description of my mother, who happens to be the perfect mom. While my dad tended to bluster, my mom would stay quiet and, behind the scenes, make certain everything was really all right. She has always been the quiet strength behind the family, although she always made sure that everyone else always got all the credit.

My mother, by the time she reached the age of fifty-five, had never officially worked a day in her life. One afternoon, she was in a very "in" restaurant—at the time—Ma Maison. She had decided that she wanted to learn how to be an expert French cook, so she asked the owner, Patrick, how she should go about it. I think she had something dilettantish in mind, such as going to France for a few weeks and taking cooking classes. Instead, Patrick told her she should go to work in the restaurant three times a week—without pay—and that in six months she'd be a great cook. That's exactly what she did. She started going in three times a week as an unpaid apprentice, and within a year, not only was she a terrific chef, she had started and was running a Ma Maison cooking school. In the twelve or so years since, she's become a queen of the LA cooking mafia, writing several respected cookbooks, working intimately with people like Wolfgang Puck, and befriending people like Julia Child and Maida Heatter. The only drawback to this is that my mother is now slightly obsessed with food. I can call up and say, "Mom, I'm a little down—I got fired from my job and my girlfriend left me and I was just run over by a truck." The odds are Mom will sympathize for a minute or so and then say, "Did I tell you about the crème brûlée I made last night? It was wonderful. I added some lemon and . . ." And she'll be off giving me instructions on how to make the perfect custard.

My mom is fairly unflappable. Nothing much seems to bother her, and especially as she's gotten more secure over the years, she always seems to take the long view and the sane view of things. A good way to illustrate the difference between the two parents is their reaction when they saw my first New York City apartment.

I suppose everyone who ever had pretensions of being an artist and who moved to New York has at one time lived in an apartment similar to mine. But, to be honest, that seems almost impossible. I think it's safe to assume that my apartment was the worst apartment ever built in New York City. It was on Perry Street near Seventh Avenue, right in the heart of Greenwich Village. It was a basement. I don't mean a basement apartment—I mean a basement. A good chunk of what was supposed to be the living room had no floor. It was just dirt and, without working too hard, you could poke around in it and peek down to the subway. When I took the place, there was no kitchen, no bathroom, not even a shower. There was also no light. The only two windows faced the street but were blocked by the building's enormous garbage cans. It also wasn't too well constructed. On particularly rainy or snowy nights, there was usually a pretty good chance that the elements would blow through the cracks in the walls. There is no feeling quite like coming home from a Greenwich Village bar at two A.M. on a snowy, icy, winter morning, crawling into bed—and finding that your sheets have been soaked through and through by snow that has been drifting into your apartment all night.

In my apartment's defense, however, it did have a great painted tin ceiling and a brick wall and a great wooden floor (the parts of it that had a floor). Also, it was right in the heart of the Village. And it was only $105 a month. Even I knew, however, that it wasn't the kind of apartment that parents love to see their child living in.

I had tried, at the time, to prepare my folks for what they were going to see when they visited New York. I found out later that for weeks beforehand, my mother had driven my father nearly mad saying things like, "Now, remember, when you see Pete's apartment, no matter what you think about it, tell him you love it." Nearly every minute of the day, according to my father, was taken up with her lectures about how important it was to me for them to support my lifestyle and my taste. Finally my father promised he would be on his best behavior and tell me he approved of where I was living—no matter what it was really like.

When it came time for them to actually see the apartment for themselves, my mother spent the entire taxi ride downtown repeating the rules to my dad. "Tell him it's great. . . . Tell him you love it. . . . Try to remember what it was like when you were young. . . ." She'd been psyching herself up for so long that when I finally heard their knock at the door and opened it to let them in, before I could say a word my mother gushed, "Oh my! It's lovely! It's perfect! Isn't it perfect? What a great apartment!" I had the presence of mind to say, "Mom, don't you want to come in and see it first before you decide if you like it?" Embarrassed, she stepped inside. My father followed. After a two-second pause, my father, looking around in wonder, blew his promise to my mother and said, "What a [dump]!"

The best description of my parents—and the difference between them—came from a director named Bill Persky, who, in a toast at one of their anniversary parties, said it was like "Adolf Hitler being married to Julie Andrews."

Adolf, Julie . . . meet Norton.

I came up to the house for dinner, Norton contentedly

hanging from my shoulder in his usual bag. I knew my father had told me not to bring him, but I was sure he didn't really mean it.

My mother made an appropriate fuss when she saw him. Not a cat lover herself, she appreciated the two things that were immediately apparent—he was great looking and so sweet-natured. She petted him delicately, not used to being around a feline. She relaxed when Norton nuzzled her hand with his nose. As he was nuzzling, my dad called down from upstairs, "Is that cat with you?" When I called up that yes, indeed, he was, the next roar was, "Well, make sure I don't see him when I come downstairs!"

After a little bit of confusion and a bit more arguing, we all finally agreed that it was impossible for me to arrange for my father never even to *see* Norton, but I did agree to try to keep him out of the way. First I tried to get my dad to understand how special this particular cat was, but he seemed to be the very first person able to resist Norton's charms.

Norton stared at him with his cutest look. He rolled over on his back, paws up in the air, inviting my father to scratch his belly. He tried rubbing up against my dad's leg. He tried snuggling up to him. Forget it. The man was ice. He truly didn't like cats, and Norton was a cat. There was no way this was ever going to be anything but an uneven truce between man and animal.

I dealt with this as best I could, although I was extremely disappointed. I felt bad that my dad couldn't open himself up to the special pleasures that Norton brought me. But clearly he couldn't.

After dinner, I took Norton back to the hotel, making sure he knew that it wasn't his fault my father didn't appreciate him. The next few days, I made my LA rounds, seeing agents, writers, film and TV people—a lot of people who called me "Babe," told me they loved me like family, and let me know I was "hot." Luckily, one agent kept me from getting a swelled head by explaining to me that it was "easy to get hot. The hard part is staying hot."

Sometimes Norton came in the car with me, sometimes he hung out at the hotel. When he was in the car, his new idea of fun, begun on the ride from San Diego, was to perch himself on my shoulder while I was driving and hang his head out my open window. By this time I had no fear that he might jump out. That just wasn't something Norton would do. Even in LA, where people are used to just about everything, I got a few interesting double takes as we were cruising around.

All in all, I decided that taking Norton from coast to coast was a simple thing to do, bound to get simpler as we both got more experienced. And just as I decided I could see no drawbacks to it, a major drawback occurred.

I got a call from my office. We were publishing a celebrity's autobiography. As is so often the case, the celebrity didn't really write the book; he just talked into a tape recorder and with a writer who was supposed to turn out a book that seemed as if it could only have been written by the celebrity himself. This is fairly common practice, as most celebrities, at least most actors and athletes, have a lot of trouble writing anything other than the words "I," "me," "mine," or "more." I had thought that this particular celebrity's book was under control. The ghostwriter had done a terrific job, the book was entertaining, and the timing was right—this lucky celebrity had managed to stay hot. But as so often happens, this famous man had gotten cold feet. When he read over his book one last time before we were to go to the printer, he decided that, even though he'd assured us every step of the way that he loved the book that bore his name, he couldn't really say all those things for the record. We'd have to cut and rewrite and drastically change things—or he wouldn't let us publish. If we tried to publish anyway, he wouldn't do any publicity, which would effectively kill any chance of selling the thing.

This charmer lived in Santa Barbara, just a couple of hours' drive from LA. Since I was already close by, the powers that be had decided that I should get in my car, head immediately up the coast, and get to work. I had five whole days to completely rewrite the book so we could meet our promised publication date.

No problem.

Scratch that . . . one problem.

Since our celebrity was already bordering on hysteria, and since I was going to be staying in his home, I didn't know what to do with Norton. My author was so deranged he could claim he was allergic to cats and throw me out of his house, killing any chance for my mission to be a success.

I could think of only one thing to do.

My mother gulped but agreed to let Norton stay in their house for the five days I was to be in Santa Barbara.

"Do you want to . . . ummm . . . check with Dad?" I asked weakly. "Just to be sure?"

"No," my courageous mother said. "I think it's better if we surprise him."

I had to agree. So, since my dad was off at a meeting, I drove Norton over to the house as quickly as possible, left even quicker, and went out to spend what I was sure would be the worst five days of my life—but which would still be better than being around my father when he found out he had to live with Norton for a week.

I was right. When I checked in that night, Mom told me it hadn't gone as well as she'd hoped. For my mother to make an admission like that meant that their house on Hazen Drive must have been something like Nagasaki the day of the bomb. She assured me, however, that Norton was still there—and was still welcome to stay.

When I called in the second night, the report was that Norton had spent some time on the couch in my parents' bedroom and that my father hadn't thrown him out.

The third night, I had been mentally beaten into a near-stupor by the aggrieved author, so I was sure I hadn't understood correctly when I heard my mother say the words "Your father told me he thought Norton was quite handsome—for a cat."

The fourth night, I figured I must be getting delirious from trying to rewrite fifty pages a day, because I was positive my mother told me, "Norton slept with us last night."

The fifth night, I was too exhausted to even call home.

I finished my rewrites somewhere around five in the morning, loaded the manuscript into my suitcase, and ran straight for my car. I arrived back in LA at seven A.M.

My mother, who usually is out of bed by six every day, was already up. I kissed her hello and nervously asked after my cat. She smiled, motioned for me to be quiet, and led me up the stairs to her and my father's bedroom. There I saw one of the greatest sights I had ever been privy to.

On the bed, sound asleep under the covers, was my father. On his chest, on top of the covers, was Norton, also sound asleep. My father's arm was curled around the top of the blanket, his hand resting gently on Norton's back.

We tiptoed out of the room, and my mother told me that, during the course of each day, Norton kept trying to get closer and closer to my dad. At first my dad shooed him away. Then, as Norton refused to give up, he began to be intrigued. As soon as the poor guy weakened, Norton went in for the kill. By their fifth night together, he had my dad petting him for hours while he sat directly on his chest. They fell asleep like that. My mom told me that my dad actually kissed Norton good night.

I had a cup of coffee and waited for the two pals to wake up. Norton was glad to see me, although not nearly as glad as he should have been. All my dad talked about was what an amazing thing it was to listen to Norton purr. "He must be happy here," he kept saying. "He purred the whole time."

"I do think he likes it here," my mother acknowledged.

The last words my dad said to me, before I drove to the airport, were, "When are you coming out here again?"

"I guess in a month or so," I told him. "Why?"

He caressed Norton. "Are you sure you don't want to leave him here until you get back?"

Major-League Assistance from "the Sisters"

Brian McRae

"T he Sisters" arrived in my home when they were only a few weeks old. I had never considered myself a cat person, but a little dark-brown, tiger-striped kitten named Monster and her black, shorthaired sister, O-fer, have turned out to be two of my best buddies. They saw me through the highs and lows of playing major-league baseball in ways I would have never thought possible.

Golfers name their pets Birdie and Bogie, so I wanted to give one of these sisters a baseball name. I decided to call the kitten with the most outgoing personality O-fer. "O" (meaning zero) is used in phrases like "0 for 1" or "0 for 2"—a way of indicating how many times a player has been up to bat without hitting the ball into the field. This isn't the kind of record a baseball player wants to have by the end of a game, but as it turned out, O-fer was a good name for a cat who helped me get through some tough times.

Monster got her name because, as a kitten, she tore up everything in sight. From an early age, she scratched more than O-fer did and was more aggressive. She would chew on newspapers, shoes, or anything else she could reach. Even now, I have to be careful not to leave the bathroom door open, or Monster will unroll toilet paper, leaving a trail of scraps all over the house. I would love to set up a video camera just to see what these two are up to while I'm gone.

When Monster and O-fer first came to live with me, the kittens didn't do a whole lot. They spent most of their time sleeping, and they were kind of boring. After about a week, they had adjusted; they started running around the house and became more interesting. They began to play games by hiding behind dressers or curling up together in one of the bottom drawers, where I would eventually find them.

I have to admit that, because I have no children, Monster and O-fer are like kids to me. I give them bottled water to drink. When I open the refrigerator, they are right there, waiting for me to feed them leftovers. They follow me around the house and sleep in my bed at night. I enjoy hanging out with the cats, playing with them for as much as a couple of hours at a time. They bring their toys to me and insist that it's playtime.

You might think that my cats' favorite toys would be the ones I buy for them, but Monster and O-fer don't play with anything conventional. Their favorite playthings are multicolored straws, shoestrings, and the plastic rings from milk bottles. I used to spend lots of money on toys, but these two cats always found something around the house they wanted to play with more.

Monster and O-fer love it when I put them out on my gated balcony, where they can soak up sunshine, watch birds fly by, and listen to the chirping. As independent-minded creatures, full of attitude, these sister cats keep me amused.

In 1997, when I played center field for the Chicago Cubs, my wife and I decided to take Monster and O-fer to Chicago with us. Because playing baseball is great when your team is winning and not so great when you're losing, the decision to bring "the Sisters" along turned out to be one of the best I ever made during my professional career. By mid-April, the Cubs were at 0 for 14. Basically, the season was over for us. But we still had many more ball games to play and a lot of disappointed fans to face. After each game, I'd return home to find Monster and O-fer waiting for me. What a relief they provided from the stress of the day or week!

Unlike other major-league sports, in which there's time off between games, just about every day is a game day in baseball; we don't have days off. A baseball team starts playing in March and continues through October. At the most, ballplayers have maybe 7 to 10 days off out of 170 to 180 days of playing. So we have the pressure of performing every day.

Time away from the game allows a player to put his mind on other things. But because we play baseball every day, one day bleeds into the next. It's like we're spending one endless day going through grinding routines, over and over again. We may be in a different city or playing against a different team, but it all seems pretty much the same. Sometimes it's as if the day never stops.

Many of the stresses and pressures that come up in a baseball season are due to traveling. We spend half of our time on the road. Major-league baseball is a mentally grueling sport because we must live out of a suitcase. A ballplayer might be in New York one day, Los Angeles the next day, and Oakland the day after that, but he is still expected to play well each day.

Because of the lack of days off and the amount of travel, a baseball player must be able to relax and regroup mentally. If you've had a bad day, you need to really shake it off, because the next day you must go out there and perform again. If you dwell on your losses, it's easy to let a bad day or two turn into a bad week. During the season, you get caught up in whether your team is playing well or not. You wonder if you're personally doing all you can do to help the team win.

Although my teammates and I were spiraling downward during the 1997 season, Monster and O-fer had no clue what I did for a living or what was going on in my time away from them. As far as they were concerned, my purpose in life was to play with them and be happy. Rolling around on the floor with Monster and O-fer put the outside world and its pressures into perspective for me. I'd find myself thinking, *Why worry?* Spending time with the cats helped me focus on what is important in the grand scheme of things. I was grateful for the gift of enjoyment with companions who didn't care what I did for a living. Monster and

O-fer didn't know if I'd had a good or bad game; it simply didn't matter to them what I did at the ballpark.

Being with Monster and O-fer in Chicago reminded me that I didn't need to be upset about a bad game. After all, how could I be angry after lying on the floor with two cats rolling around on top of me, tugging at my ears, and licking my fingers? When I came home from a game, I threw straws and milk rings, and they ran and brought these favorite toys back to me. I relaxed by brushing and grooming the cats and clipping their back claws. When they were younger, it had been a big ordeal to bathe them. But as they got older, the cats learned to like playing with water, and they enjoyed splashing it from the sink. Whenever I took a bath, they liked to sit on the edge of the bathtub and poke their paws in my bath water.

Playing with Monster and O-fer caused me to realize that I could get joy from things other than baseball. Even when something didn't go my way at work, the cats made me happy. They didn't ask questions; they didn't pass judgment. Their companionship allowed me to separate work from home.

Lots of ballplayers can't do that. If they have one bad day, it leads to two bad days, then to three, and finally to an entire bad week. The game consumes them. Monster and O-fer were a good diversion for me. I often thought that if other ballplayers had buddies like these two cats, they would have an easier time handling the ups and downs of baseball.

Even though Monster and O-fer get mad and ignore

me when I've been away for a while, they seem to know when I need attention, and they're more than willing to give it to me. If they see me resting on the couch, they can tell if I'm not feeling well. Then they come up and quietly lie on my lap. It's one of the most comforting feelings in the world.

Many changes occur in baseball and in life, but one thing I can count on is that Monster and O-fer are always there for me.

Meant for
Each Other

Ann Kindig

I 'd thought my life was complete: marriage, two healthy sons, a house filled with books. And then, when our sons were in college, my thirty-year marriage ended in divorce and left me feeling totally rejected and unlovable.

My face in the mirror became a gloomy reminder of what I'd lost. Family and friends were supportive, but I felt a huge void in my life. I prayed to feel whole again.

One day a friend telephoned to tell me that an elderly neighbor had gone to a nursing home and had been forced to leave his Manx cat behind. "I thought of you immediately," my friend said. But I wasn't interested in taking on a cat.

Later the phone rang again: "I know of a cat who needs a home," another friend said. "A Manx . . ."

A Manx? The kind that doesn't have a tail? Why should I want a cat without a tail? I politely declined.

To keep busy I attended divorce-recovery workshops, shopped with friends who told me to change my image, sat through seminars, and read self-help books by the dozen. The face in my mirror reflected newly improved makeup but little joy.

Then yet another friend called. "Have I told you about this cat named Twink?" she said. "She's a Manx who—"

All right, all right, if people were so determined to give me a Manx, maybe I should see one. A meeting was arranged, and I was less than awed. Twink was black as midnight, fat, and dumpy. Her back legs were so long that they made her seem to lumber, and when she walked, her stomach swayed from side to side. And she wasn't really tailless—she had a little corkscrew of a stub.

Twink, I learned, had been abandoned at a resort and taken to a shelter, where workers couldn't bear to destroy her. Then along came the elderly gentleman who took her in. When he left his home, Twink was alone again, and that's where my friends came into the picture. And the amazing thing I discovered was that not one of the three friends who called me knew that the others were suggesting that Twink and I were meant for each other.

"Okay, I'll take her," I said finally. It seemed to me that God wanted me to have this cat.

Twink came into my home, sniffed around, then methodically rubbed her scent on everything from the furniture to the flowerpots. Then she defended her territory in a noisy nose-to-nose-through-the-glass confrontation with Gertrude, the huge orange cat from next door. But it wasn't until I awoke at night and found her pressed against my side that I comprehended that I was the one who had been adopted.

Now I grew curious about this special kind of cat, and I

was particularly pleased with a story someone told me about Twink's lack of tail. "When the Manx cat hurried to board Noah's Ark," a friend explained, "Noah accidentally shut the door on its tail!"

I hadn't anticipated that my home life would turn into a slapstick routine, with Twink galloping to greet me at the door. It was difficult to stay depressed when Twink sprawled like an ape to groom herself, tumbled over like a beanbag when she wanted her stomach scratched, and made Tarzan-like noises as she bounded onto my bed. At night Twink snuggled in my lap while I read, her stubby non-tail twitching in time with her contented purr.

And gradually as I laughed at Twink, I began to laugh in the rest of my life. I took on some new duties at work and helped organize some projects that excited me at church. Life was good again.

Then came the morning that Twink and I watched as Gertrude, the neighbor cat, sauntered across our outside deck. As Twink crouched at the patio door with hackles raised, Gertrude decided to show off. Turning and twisting with the grace of a matador, she swished her fluffy tail like a cape. Twink was infuriated, but I was amused. "Don't pay any attention to her, Twink," I said. "That long tail serves no purpose at all. Who needs it anyway?"

Who needs it anyway? Slowly I saw the connection. A part of my life was gone now; at one time it had been a wonderful part. But just as Twink could carry on without a tail, I could have a happy life without a marriage.

Twink was whole, and her lack of a tail made her no less so. And now I knew why the face in my mirror had been smiling so much lately: I was whole too. The answer to my prayer had come in the form of a cat who walked like an Angus steer, ate like a pig, and lounged around like an orangutan.

Once I'd thought my life was complete. Well, it was still complete. Noah might have shut the door on the Manx's tail—but God hadn't shut his door on either one of us.

Clawed's Story:
The Older Cat

Anitra Frazier with Norma Eckroate

I've always been a great one for adopting elderly cats. Most people want kittens, but I guess I just got an overdose of that great American urge to fight for the underdog—or the undercat, as the case may be.

Over the past twelve years, my apartment has been host to dozens of "undercats" of the geriatric variety who lounge about, enjoying their sunset days. The cats all came burdened with particular physical ailments and have paid their bills by giving me new knowledge as I tried to solve their problems.

Old Clawed Quincy was the cat who taught me the most. He was my very first geriatric cat. Coming from a background of neglect, as he did, he was a regular walking textbook of elderly-cat ailments. Also, because of him, I was faced for the first time with a delicate moral dilemma that I had, up to that point in my relatively new career as a cat-care professional, managed to avoid.

Clawed lived the first fifteen years of his life with the Quincys, a wealthy and intellectual family of four. He had once been cherished, loved, and appreciated, but that was many years ago. The two boys were young then, and Clawed had arrived as a tiny white fluff ball curled up inside a shoebox under the Christmas tree. As far as I could piece the story together, there had followed many happy years of adventure and fun. Clawed slept night after blissful night curled close beside a youngster's ear, and in the mornings there was always romping under the sheets.

Childhood diseases came and went, and Clawed rose to these occasions with soothing purrs and gentle washings with a tongue that scratched and tickled young wrists and fingers. Obviously Clawed felt deeply his responsibility to this human family.

A real pedigreed Persian, Clawed was the pride of the household. He had long, snow-white fur and huge copper eyes that sparkled like new pennies most of the time. But that, as I said, was many years ago.

Now the children were grown and gone away to school, the parents were immersed in their own careers, and Clawed had become a sort of retired cat. No one had paid him much attention for the past few years until, this winter, it was discovered that copious amounts of dandruff had appeared in his fur and were being shed all over the furniture and the rugs. The busy Quincys had neither the time nor the patience to clean up after a cat who was no longer an integral part of the household, and so, at this point, just before Clawed's fifteenth Christmas, I was called in to "give him a bath or something!"

Mr. Quincy, tall and distinguished, greeted me at the door and, after taking my overcoat and boots, he led me in to

166

the exquisitely appointed living room, where an equally exquisite Mrs. Quincy smiled, grasped my hand, and gestured in the direction of the sofa.

"And this is Clawed," she caroled gaily.

At the sound of her voice, a dull white mound under the end table began to stir and unfold, and a sad little face peeked diffidently out at me.

"Clawed's been a naughty boy, getting dandruff and hair all over the apartment," she cooed, wagging her finger in Clawed's direction. "Miss Anitra's going to get you all nice and clean now, Clawed."

The uppermost thought in my mind was that dandruff was probably the least of Clawed's problems. To begin with, those big copper eyes were exuding a nasty brown discharge, and, as the cat began wobbling unsteadily to his feet, I could see that his front legs were slightly deformed. His ankles buckled badly inward with his weight back on his heels. The toes, I observed, were flopping softly out to each side. As he stood there, swaying ever so gently, a look of polite inquiry on his face, he reminded me of an elderly ballet master with fallen arches. Clawed was definitely not a well cat.

I picked the old boy up and carried him very gently out to the kitchen counter. Bones were all I could feel—no muscle tone, no firm flesh. Then, as I began stroking my fingers through the sparse hair, examining the oily skin, Clawed gave a yawn and stretched himself out full length on the counter; he trusted me. I hadn't combed him more than three strokes when a magnificent purr came rumbling out of that bedraggled old body to fill the Quincys' shiny kitchen with the sound of a cat's contentment. Clawed was obviously hungry for affection.

Old Clawed relaxed into those warm suds like a tired executive. When I began the deep massage, he looked up, gave me a long, blissful blink, and lowered his purr to a murmur. Mr. and Mrs. Quincy were enjoying the whole scene to the hilt, so I decided to seize the opportunity and ask a few pertinent questions about their cat's sorry state.

That was when I was told about Clawed's "retired status," which explained his depressed attitude. I also discovered that the diet they were providing consisted mainly of one of those dry foods that are supposed to be so wonderful because they are "low in ash." The Quincys served it in one of those automatic dispensers which was left available twenty-four hours a day. So I had an explanation for the dandruff as well. In former days, it seems, when the kids were in charge of Clawed's menu, their idea of a high-class diet for a high-class cat had been nothing but sliced roast beef and turkey. This is a terrific beginning, but hardly what one could call balanced nutrition, since there was no roughage, no bulk. He would probably be suffering from constipation. Since there was very little calcium in sliced meats, he would probably have porous bones as well, hence the buckling ankles. To top it all off, his kidneys would probably be exhausted from the protein imbalance. Failing kidneys is a sure cause of dandruff. And, incidentally, Clawed hadn't seen the inside of a veterinarian's office in nigh on to seven years.

I pointed out to the Quincys that Clawed missed their attention. To illustrate this, I asked Mrs. Quincy to hold his head and stroke his throat during the blow drying. Old Clawed was floating on cloud nine. His eyes were squinting in an ecstasy of sensual pleasure and he was making crooked little ineffectual kneading motions with his feet on the towel. He obviously adored the lady.

When I broached the subject of a higher quality diet, I encountered a blank wall. Feline nutrition was definitely not within the Quincys' realm of interest. I gently pointed out that Clawed's teeth badly needed cleaning, and I was relieved when they said, "Well, he might as well have that done, and get a thorough examination at the same time."

"We'd rather pay for the veterinarian than spend a lot of time fussing with food," Mrs. Quincy explained. "It's easier." Obviously what was "easier" for Clawed hadn't entered their minds. Before I left, I myself made an appointment for Clawed to see Dr. McAlister the very next day. I was hoping that, if the facts were presented by a veterinarian, then the Quincys might finally agree that some major dietary and lifestyle changes should be made.

I made sure that they had my telephone number, and I suggested they call me after they saw the doctor, because then I could design a diet based on her diagnosis and we could help Old Clawed get back at least some of his former health and beauty. I was finding Old Clawed irresistible, and I just could not imagine how anybody else wouldn't feel exactly the same way.

Two days went by and I didn't hear from the Quincys. I thought about Clawed, sweet Old Clawed sitting proudly atop the hassock after his blow drying, a new cat. Without a change of diet and at least a little bit of TLC, Clawed would very rapidly revert to being a very old cat again.

"Forget Clawed," I told myself. "A lack of professional detachment leads to emotional exhaustion." I used to collect truisms my first few years on the job. I soon learned, however, that they are easier said than done, and, as Day Two drew to a close, I had decided that professional detachment need not necessarily prohibit a tiny bit of professional curiosity. So I put in a call to the veterinarian's office and had the receptionist pull out Clawed's card and read me the data entered by Dr. McAlister. Clawed had been found to be about eighty-five percent deaf, a common enough state of affairs in old cats who have been on a poor diet. It was nothing to get too excited about. However, he was also arthritic in his lower spine and both hip joints. He had been found to have severe rickets in all four legs and, to top it all off, just as I feared, his kidneys were all shriveled up, with very little function left.

Clawed's body was breaking down, but none of these conditions were irreversible. Arthritic deposits in and around the joints can slowly be dissolved. Kidney tissue can be healed and slowly regenerate. Weak and porous bones can be recalcified and strengthened again. Clawed could still look forward to several years of quiet pleasure, warm and secure in the midst of the family he loved.

A total of four days dragged by and Clawed's owners still

hadn't called me. The pre-Christmas rush of bathing requests had me zooming all over town on my bike. The temperature was hovering up in the forties and I hoped it would hold. In spare moments at home, I kept my mind directed toward positive pursuits, crocheting the woolen mouse toys that I was giving as Christmas presents that year. But, try as I might, I could not get Old Clawed out of my mind.

"Worrying over something about which you can do nothing is a shameful waste of energy," I reminded myself. But still my thoughts kept running back to Old Clawed and the Quincys.

"Maybe they forgot," I told myself. "Maybe they didn't want to bother me. Maybe they lost my number." I gave in and called them about an hour after dinner on the fourth day.

Mr. Quincy answered and said right away that they had just been talking about calling me. I breathed a sigh of relief, but I wasn't relieved for long. Clawed's condition had gotten worse. The dandruff was back as bad as ever and all he did, said Mr. Quincy, was sleep, drink the water dish dry, and run to the litter box.

I began to explain to Mr. Quincy that these were all symptoms of failing kidneys, which would improve to a surprising extent as soon as we got his diet in hand, but he cut me short and then began to beat about the bush. First he told me how they'd always wanted the best for Old Clawed; then about how busy they both were and how lonely it must be for Old Clawed now that the children were gone; and how a cat couldn't be happy anyway with all that messy dandruff all over his skin.

And then, finally, he came to the point. Mr. Quincy wanted to know if I would be so kind as to come over, pick up Clawed, and "drop him off" at the veterinarian's office to be put to sleep.

So there it was. Sometimes I argue for the cat and sometimes, when I sense that it won't do any good anyway, I don't. This was, I felt, a case where the owner's mind was firmly closed. The Quincys had obviously concocted some pretty fancy rationalizations to support this decision; the last thing they wanted to listen to now was facts.

The sort of commitment in time and effort that Clawed needed was not what the Quincys had bargained for fifteen years ago when they bought their children a little white fluff ball. They hadn't thought about it then, and they didn't want to think about it now.

I didn't want to think about it either. My mind was in a state of semi-shock. I wanted to hang up because I needed a few moments to handle what was happening. So I told Mr. Quincy I'd be over right away.

I took a taxi. The temperature was dropping. Crossing Eighty-sixth Street, I watched the Christmas shoppers leaning into the wind, blinking away the snowflakes that were swirling into their faces; and I tried to prepare my mind for what I had to do next.

"At least," I told myself, "Clawed won't be left alone to die slowly of neglect and loneliness." Clawed, who purred when you touched him. I quickly turned my thoughts away from the purring and concentrated on the snow and the frost forming on the cab window.

When I arrived at the Quincys', I found that they seemed to want to get the thing over as quickly as possible, for when Mr. Quincy opened the door he had the carrier in hand with Clawed huddled dismally inside. As he handed the case over to me, there was no sound from Clawed. He was just a weight, a weight that was much too light, transferred into my hands.

Mr. Quincy tried to speak, failed, and then said, much too loudly, "How much do you . . . how much should . . . how much is it?"

The emotions I saw on his face were many. But under it all I saw guilt, guilt that he couldn't face and would never admit to. And I knew very clearly, in the same moment that I accepted that old cat's weight, that this man would have to live with that guilt for the rest of his life. Poor man, if he ever did come to an understanding of what he had done, it would be too late.

I retreated into my businesslike manner. "I'll take care of everything," I said. "I'll hold Clawed when he's put to sleep so that he won't be with strangers. Dr. McAlister can bill you for the injection and cremation. As far as my fee is concerned, I work by the hour. My fee is the same as it was for grooming. I'll send you a bill." It was a relief when the door closed.

Down in the lobby, the doorman suggested I have a seat while he went out to look for a cab. Snow flew like ash around the doorman's black umbrella. As I sat there hugging Clawed's carrier and watching the big white flakes settle and melt, settle and melt, certain moral questions began breaking through into my conscious mind, clamoring to be resolved.

I had performed this service before, but always it had been for clients I knew well and only after long and careful consultation with the doctor. It had always been after we knew for certain that life was unpleasant for our friend and that we had no hope of bringing him comfort again. If Clawed was not in pain, if he was still capable of enjoying such pleasures as the bath and blow drying and petting and massage and attention, and food, was it then morally correct to put him to death? On the other hand, his owners were not prepared to give him any of these pleasures. Clawed was not my cat, and I had given my word to his owners that I would carry out their wish.

Fate had brought Clawed and me together. At least now there was a loving and responsible person in charge, I told myself, someone who could make sure that Clawed would be secure and comfortable and relaxed all the way through to the end.

I knew perfectly well that every day thousands of young, healthy cats are routinely destroyed by animal shelters simply because there is no room for them. It was highly unprofessional to become emotionally upset over one sick old specimen simply because he and I had become briefly acquainted. Years before I had wrestled with the question of taking a life—something which can't be given back—and had finally come to the conclusion that terminal suffering should be cut short. But was Clawed suffering? And even if he were, was his condition actually terminal, or could a caring person give him a few extra days, or weeks, or months of quiet pleasure? And then there I was, back at square one—the owners were not willing to do it. My professional detachment had evaporated and blown away by the time the doorman was back to announce the arrival of my taxi.

As I seated myself inside and started to tell my driver my destination, the crowning blunder of the evening dawned on me: Dr. McAlister's office was long closed for the night, and here I was with a sick old cat in my lap. There was only one thing left to do; I would just have to take Clawed home with me until tomorrow.

"Until tomorrow" . . . what a laugh. Clawed was destined to spend a contented four *years* with me. In the end, the moral quandary really boiled down to only one thing: Was Clawed in pain?

The next day, after Dr. McAlister had finished a thorough geriatric workup, I asked her straight out. "Is Clawed in any pain?"

"Pain, no." She gently palpated his lower back above the hip socket. "His kidneys are not causing pain. He will have an occasional twinge of arthritis, of course, and there is a nasty gum infection caused by that filthy tartar, but overall he is simply tired. The kidney disease, the bone porosity, these things are serious of course, but they're not giving him any actual pain. He's just old, Anitra. Do you understand? He's just terribly old."

He was also terribly loving, and terribly outgoing, and warm, and responsive, and purring like a buzz saw as he lounged there on that metal examining table.

I had made up my mind to a course of action, and I had a strong hunch that Dr. McAlister would probably go along with me on it. "Okay," I said, "just suppose I were to take him home for a while, and give him a nice quiet place and supply him with all the nutrients his body needs, to repair the kidneys and strengthen the bones."

Dr. McAlister was shifting into her lecturing pose, so I grabbed a quick breath and hurried on. "I know I promised the Quincys I'd put him to sleep, but I never said *when* I'd do it. Well, just look at him." I gestured to Clawed who was, thankfully, blinking trustfully up at Dr. McAlister and still purring in his most resonant tones.

Dr. McAlister sighed and shook her head, but she didn't say no, so I pressed my advantage.

"Now I know you can't clean his teeth because his kidneys aren't strong enough to stand the anesthetic. But suppose you were to clean just one tooth, one a month. Then you wouldn't need anesthesia. I'll bring him in once a month and you can scale one or two teeth and you can check his progress at the same time. You and I will keep a close watch on him, and whenever you tell me that things are getting too uncomfortable for him, well, then we can put him to sleep.

Dr. McAlister was opening Clawed's mouth again, muttering "filthy, just filthy," as she carefully worked the tooth scaler in between a chunk of grayish yellow tartar and the gum line. Then, with a firm downward pressure, she dislodged the piece onto her waiting index finger and flung it into the metal tray. Success! But before I could press my advantage further, she held up her hand. "All right, Anitra, all right. I suppose you can give it a try if you want to."

"I want to," I said.

So Clawed was mine now, and I had to admit that it was really what I'd wanted all along.

The night before, when Clawed and I had shown up at the apartment, Purr, Florence, and Priscilla had made no objections to the sudden addition of a house guest. This was probably because the bewildered cat I lifted out of the carrying case was at such a low energy level that even my imaginative Florence couldn't pretend that he posed any sort of a threat to her position as reigning queen of the household. In fact, introducing a new cat to the household turned out to be no problem at all. For this I was grateful, since by that time I was feeling just about as tired as Clawed looked.

As soon as I lifted Clawed out onto the floor, he spotted my little keyhole desk up against the radiator and made straight for that. He padded into the opening, circled once around, the tips of his fur brushing the hot radiator and, unable to bend his legs sufficiently to achieve a graceful landing, collapsed with a plop onto the floor. His eyes were full of confusion and sadness, and he didn't look as if he could get up enough spirit to take a drink of water.

Big Purr, who was still young enough to be thrilled, glided over to investigate Clawed's extended hind foot. He stopped, nose suspended about one millimeter from the upturned pad, and sniffed. Clawed didn't respond. His chin rested softly on his paws, his eyes staring at nothing in particular. Clawed was in mourning. For fifteen years he had loved the Quincys. He loved them now, as always, and he seemed to sense somehow that he was not going to see them again, not ever. He didn't know any of the "why's"—but why didn't matter to Clawed. Nothing at all mattered anymore.

"Stress can kill a cat." I've heard veterinarians say it again and again. I would have to deal with Clawed's mental state before I even began to tackle his physical problems, and the first order of business would be a "Snug Retreat."

Sacrificing one of my storage boxes, a nice sturdy Schweppes carton, I emptied the summer blouses out of it onto the dresser. I'd have to get myself another carton tomorrow. I moved Clawed onto the sofa and, laying the box on its side, I slid it in under the desk up against the radiator. Pulling out one of the desk drawers, I clipped onto it a 75-watt grow light and directed the warmth right into the box. Then I got Old Clawed from the sofa and slid him into his Snug Retreat.

I would estimate that, in the weeks that followed, Clawed snoozed away about twenty-one out of every twenty-four hours in there. The Snug Retreat is a little bit of heaven on earth for an arthritic old cat with failing kidneys.

Priscilla, my lovely Blue Point Siamese, observed all this from her lofty perch atop the bookcase. At age fifteen she had achieved a fine philosophical detachment and was quite content to let sleeping cats lie. That night my own three "furry purries" slept as usual in the bed with me.

But the luscious warmth of the Snug Retreat drew my little Priscilla like a magnet. No Siamese can resist it for long, even if there is a large and strange cat sleeping inside. Before long Priscilla's perfect little gray body could frequently be seen lying next to Clawed's bony one. Priscilla's figure was exquisite, her coat shining and soft. I had to keep reminding myself, "Priscilla and Clawed are the same age."

Priscilla had come to me when she was twelve. She was a petite, cobby little Blue Point Siamese—the old-fashioned type, not inbred. At that time she was moderately healthy despite a poor diet in her previous home. Now, after three years of work on my part, she looked more like a crown princess than a middle-aged queen. I wondered how much time I had left to work on Clawed. Fifteen-year-olds are slower to improve than twelve-year-olds.

"Nature heals," I reminded myself, "if only we give her the tools to work with." And as an all-around tool for nursing care, you certainly can't beat the Snug Retreat. Besides providing a place where a cat can "get away from it all," the steady warmth reduces the number of calories a cat needs to burn just to maintain body heat. Also, the light waves in the grow-light spectrum are closer to those of natural, or full-spectrum, light.

I am convinced that many elderly animals become increasingly vulnerable to various fungi and skin parasites partly because they tend to lie in dark places seeking warmth and quiet. Back in the days when I was working in a veterinarian's office, I had become aware that parasites such as ringworm and mites were most often found on elderly and/or diseased animals. In fact, I came to regard parasites as a veritable lurking menace for the older cat. Clawed's low vitality made him a prime candidate for fungal infestations, and with four cats to care for now, as well as a burgeoning business to run, I did not need a ringworm outbreak to make my life complete.

Years later, I improved on the Snug Retreat by following the advice of Dr. Richard Pitcairn, author of *Dr. Pitcairn's Complete Guide to Natural Health for Dogs and Cats*. I installed a full-spectrum light from the health-food store under my desk. It gives all the light frequencies of sunlight. Since it's a cool light, I also used a regular 75-watt bulb for its warmth. I must insert a word of caution here: Never use a sunlamp on a cat, or any other animal for that matter. Those ultraviolet rays are much too strong, and even a short exposure can cause blindness.

I went out on the bike every day, paying grooming calls around town. The snow gets cleared away pretty quickly in New York. The snowplows are poised and ready to sweep away the bulk of it in half a day. Then by sundown the traffic has done the rest. As long as there was no wind or ice, I would ride. I prefer to be out in the fresh air. Every night when I returned to the apartment, everyone would run to the door to greet me and sniff the cold and damp from my fingers and boots—everyone, that is, except Clawed.

Clawed was too deaf to hear the commotion we were making and too deep in dreams to smell the gust of fresh air I brought in with me, and so I would greet the others and then seek out Old Clawed in his Snug Retreat.

Since he was deaf, I would always announce myself by rapping my knuckles three times on the floor near his foot. That way I got his attention and alerted him to my presence before I actually touched him. I didn't want to startle his old nerves.

The freezing weather lasted into the next week, but luckily Clawed was in no further need of veterinary care. When Clawed first arrived he could barely make it to the litter box and back again. Eating was an effort. Everything was a big project for him, and after each project, he'd sleep and sleep—Nature's prescription for healing.

I had started Clawed on a high-carbohydrate diet to improve his kidney function, and I was slipping in the appropriate vitamins so that Nature would have as much ammunition to work with as possible.

He had to be force-fed for the first few days because he was so weak, but he was a cooperative patient, almost too cooperative. I kept wishing he would exhibit some show of will, but apparently he needed more time. So I just let his body absorb the new diet while he snoozed away that first month, and I waited for the signs that would tell me that Clawed's system was changing gears.

During his few waking hours, I let him know again and again that we were glad he was with us. Old cats like Clawed need frequent demonstrations of love. I sometimes wonder if they feel they are somehow lacking in appeal because they can no longer amuse us with lively antics or impress us with their athletic leaps. Whatever the reason, many older cats withdraw into themselves; they don't overtly call for attention as once they did. So it's up to the kindly owner to be sensitive to this subtle change and to make the overture himself. I found that it was altogether too easy for me to forget to do this for Clawed because I was so busy and the old boy so withdrawn. During his last few years with the Quincys, he had been conditioned to believe that the only good cat was an inconspicuous cat. So the only way to be sure that I was fulfilling his need for more affection was to consciously incorporate it into some activity I was already doing. For example, when I was sitting at the desk answering telephone messages from my clients, I would reach down and give Clawed a little head stroke at the end of each conversation. If I was writing, I did this at the end of each page.

Old cats, like kittens, sleep very soundly. Sleeping like the dead was a perfect description of Clawed's slumber. More than once I gently tapped his box and stroked him to rouse him slightly, just so I could be sure he was still with us.

By the end of the second week, Clawed was eating on his own. He would pad over to the food dish, stumble to a halt, and sway dangerously on his weak legs as he gulped his meal. He ate as fast as possible so as to finish it off before he fell down. After witnessing this performance twice, I moved his bowl close to the wall, where he discovered that a cat could lean for support and munch away at a more dignified pace.

Getting in and out of the litter box was like climbing Mt. Everest for Clawed. But once inside, he learned to use the old "lean against the wall" technique again. However, several times he didn't have the energy to make it out again, and I came upon him sleeping peacefully in a corner of the litter box, his head propped up against the side. I scooped him up, held him and rocked him and nuzzled him; and, every time, he would look up at me and give me that old squint of pleasure, and his purr would crescendo until I felt my own body vibrating with his. I found myself picking him up and rocking him quite a lot. That squint and that purr were my first signs that we had a chance for success. A cat who can purr like that is certainly not a cat who has given up on life.

After one month on the kidney-building diet, the urine began to have a smell again, evidence that the kidneys were beginning to function as the waste-disposal organs they are. Now Clawed was able to make it in and out of the litter box by himself every time.

Going into the second month, I noticed that Clawed was staying awake more. He would prop his chin on those big floppy front paws and watch with benign pleasure while Purr and Florence pursued a rollicking game of soccer, his round copper eyes gazing in wonder as their dented Ping-Pong ball went bouncing crazily across the hardwood floor.

I decided that he was ready for a little exercise, so I began placing him on his feet after our cuddle sessions as opposed to laying him right down in the box. After a week I began increasing the distance he would have to walk to get back to his box until, finally, I had him trekking a good ten feet three times a day. Afterward, he'd flop himself down under the warm light and sleep like the dead for the next few hours. I had to walk the fine line between exercise and overexertion. I judged that three short sessions a day would be easier on an old body than one long one.

Massage gives physical contact and a demonstration of love that even a deaf or blind animal can appreciate and enjoy. Remembering Clawed's joyful response that last time I groomed him at the Quincys, I made my stroking down his back firmer and stronger, using Clawed's response to guide me in how much pressure to use.

It was the daily grooming ritual that was the first "family activity" in which Clawed was able to participate fully. Of course, a few alterations in the grooming ritual had to be made to tailor it especially for Clawed's needs. The older cat's skin is extremely delicate and lacks almost all of its youthful elasticity. Combing and brushing must be done with a lighter and slower hand, especially for a cat as thin and bony as Clawed was. For Purr, Florence, and Priscilla I used the small slicker brush. But for Clawed I used the Resco wide-tooth comb. I made each stroke quite slow to insure that I would never knock the comb accidentally against a protruding bone. Old cats are delicate.

My next step was to find out whether or not Clawed would be able to use his shoulder and back muscles again. I wanted him to begin reaching out with his front legs. So, after his cuddle sessions, instead of placing him lightly down on the floor, I began stopping him with his feet just an inch or so above the floor. His instinctive reaction was to wiggle a tiny bit and stretch his front legs forward as he tried to complete the descent. "Bravo, Clawed!" I'd say, and lower him to a touchdown, front feet first. Clawed's body was beginning to function smoothly again; it was a safe bet that the alkalizing vegetables I was using in the food were doing away with some of the arthritic deposits.

Unfortunately, Clawed and I had only recently met. If I had known him for a few years, I would have had yet another very powerful tool at my disposal, the use of old established rituals.

I encourage owners of older cats to continue any ritual activity that they and their cat have enjoyed over the years. The game of "chase the sash" before meals or the morning snuggle and romp under the sheets takes on a new value in the declining years. These things give a cat a feeling of security and continuity, as well as providing beneficial exercise.

Here in New York I know many sedate elderly cats who take an evening stroll up and down the apartment house hallway. This decorous and gentle activity began originally when the cats were very young. In the old days it could have included a scamper pell-mell down the hall after a ball or a tussle in front of the elevators with a furry feline neighbor. I encourage owners to continue the ritual of the hallway stroll, most especially in the later years. It makes a cat feel young again. It gives him a reason to get up and out of that warm box, move about a bit, and get the circulation going.

Naturally, a few alterations will have to be made in any game or ritual as the cat ages. You will have to be clever, and make these changes in such a way that the cat will never suspect that he is deficient or lacking in any way. If the exercise involves a game of chasing and catching something, you will have to become very skillful at engineering the game so that your cat will still "win" as often as he did before. Do you remember when he was a youngster, how quick you had to be to keep the sash away from him or to keep him from catching the ball on the first bounce? Now you must pull the sash a bit slower. Don't let him win all the time—there should still be a bit of a challenge there, but do be sure that he wins, at the very least, every other time. After all, the experience of success has great psychological benefit. And be sure to praise his cleverness, his grace and quickness. Tell him you're proud of him and that you wish you were as skilled as he is. The latest scientific findings show that cats and dogs can "read" your thought concepts, so don't lie—be sincere in your praise.

Clawed's water dish and special litter box were right beside my desk and, because failing kidneys cause frequent drinking and copious urination, I cleaned his box four to six times a day. If I had to be out for several hours at a time, I left two litter boxes there for him to use.

The bladder and kidneys of any older cat are not what they used to be, so, especially if your home includes stairs, it's wise to make the litter box more convenient than ever.

I must, in all fairness, give credit to my feline coworkers for the part they played in Clawed's eventual recovery. After all, they took him in and nurtured him just as much as I did, each in his or her own way.

Purr has always been my cat-in-chief. That first night he demonstrated his acceptance of Clawed by showing off and proclaiming his territories. The fact that he was communicating with Clawed at all sent a subliminal signal to my two females that Clawed was allowed to stay. Purr is innately generous.

For her part, Priscilla always displayed impeccable etiquette when she snuggled into the Snug Retreat; she would reach her nose close to Clawed's ear and breathe softly to announce her arrival. When Clawed opened his eyes or lifted his head, she would then lick his forehead two or three times, begging permission to stay. After Clawed had given her his eye contact of welcome, she would then settle in with perfect grace, her soft, warm little body snuggled up against Clawed's arthritic hip joints. Priscilla was a lady.

Florence was a wonderful diversion. She is such a ditsy little ding-a-ling that not even Old Clawed could take her seriously. But she was the one who ultimately made Clawed feel really at home, really a part of the family.

It happened one morning when spring was in the air. I wanted to put in the kitchen window screen so that all of us could enjoy the fresh air, and so I did, which delayed the morning feeding. Florence, feeling impatient, jumped up on the counter to cheer me on and, as usual, I gently but firmly shoved her off. She leaped for the floor but, unfortunately, this time Clawed's tail was lying across her touchdown point, and so Florence landed squarely on the tail.

Clawed yelled with surprise, startling Florence. She responded by hitting him in the head, and Clawed countered with bared teeth and a hiss right in her face. Florence flounced off, declaring in loud Siamese cacophony how insulted she was.

And I, who witnessed the little spat, was happy as a lark. No cat is truly part of a group until he has a little tiff with another group member about something. Clawed had finally expressed himself and in very strong terms, and it was ding-a-ling Florence who gave him that opportunity. For me it was that longed-for signal that Clawed had finally come out of retirement.

Feeding the
Multitudes

Thirza Peevey

Like most small-town newspapers, ours did not often have much news to report. After talking about the crops and the weather, telling whose kids got an award in school that week, and throwing in a few recipes, there wasn't much else to say. To fill the required six pages, the reporters often went looking for unusual animals, precocious kids, and phenomena of nature. On one particular day when I was young, the headline in the *Daily Statesman* proclaimed the little calico cat belonging to the local County Judge Executive to be the best mouser in the county. The small article that accompanied her picture detailed a few of her exploits and mentioned that she had kittens that were looking for a home.

I didn't think much about the story until the next day. When my aunt and uncle stopped by, I noticed movement in the cab of the truck they had parked under our maple tree. Suddenly the sweetest little pixie-face of an eight-week-old tortoiseshell kitten popped up into view. They had gotten one of those kittens for themselves.

I was instantly captivated by the kitten. Before anyone

could stop me, I had her out of the truck and into my arms. We bonded the moment we touched. I carried her around and played with her all evening. When John and Fran left, the kitten stayed with me. No one had the heart to take her away from me.

Skeeter (because she wasn't any bigger than a mosquito) quickly became part of the family. She was a runty, stunted little thing, but made up for it in personality. She was quite the hunter, as her celebrity mother had been, and she soon began cleaning up the inevitable mice and rats that gather on a farm to gobble up livestock feed. She was always around the front porch the moment she heard the door open and wanted to sit on any lap that presented itself. Her silly antics kept us in stitches.

That same summer, our neighbor's marmalade cat decided she liked our house better than theirs. We kept taking her home, but she wouldn't stay. Eventually our neighbors got another cat and Josephine became ours. Not that we really needed another cat. As with any farm cat, Josie had many kittens. Farming isn't exactly a way to get rich, and we could barely afford to keep afloat, let alone get the cats spayed. The refrain from an old children's book began spinning in my head: "Hundreds of cats, thousands of cats, millions and billions and trillions of cats." When Skeeter came of age, she only added more kittens to our quandary.

Once Josie's kittens were old enough to be weaned, we started offering them to friends, relatives, and visiting salesmen. The man who sold us our tractor offered to take Josie to catch the mice in his shop. When his children fell in love with the kittens, he let them each pick one. The other four little tom kittens were lost without mama, but not for long. You see, Skeeter's mama had passed along to her the instinct that made her such a great mouser. No, it wasn't good eyesight or hearing. It wasn't great balance or powerful muscles. It was kindness and generosity. Skeeter just called the kittens over and made room for four more along with her three. She nursed those four, bathed them, and caught mice for them just as she did for her own. Out of those two litters, we kept a little female we called Yolanda and Josie's four little tom kittens: Matthew, Charlie Pinguely, Figero, and Oscar.

Yolanda was the prettiest cat I think I have ever seen, before or since. She was nearly the spitting image of her mother, except that wherever Skeeter was black and orange, Yolanda was grey tabby and orange tabby. She had the same sweet face, with a perfect Y between her ears, hence the name. If anything, all the positive qualities of her mother and grandmother were concentrated in Yolanda. Where Skeeter was sweet and affectionate, Yolanda was sweeter and more affectionate. Where Skeeter was generous, Yolanda was more so. Where Skeeter was a good hunter, Yolanda was better.

Yolanda eventually had a litter of kittens herself, the proud father being no less than Oscar, one of Josephine's boys that Skeeter had raised alongside of Yolanda.

Now that she was a mother, Yolanda took the responsibilities of a huntress quite seriously. She was good at it, and she knew it. Several times a day the rural silence was broken by the sound of mama cat calling her babies to come and eat. With all that practice, her skills grew sharper and sharper.

At first it was mice and other small creatures, but by the time she had her second litter the next summer, she graduated to catching larger wildlife. The blessing with Yolanda was that she never had more than one litter of three kittens per year. She never stopped feeding the first litter when the second was born. So now she was feeding a litter of year-old cats and a litter of baby kittens. Soon she was feeding so many mouths that even her hunting skills weren't enough. She learned to steal eggs from the hens and carry them carefully from the lower barn to the house, nearly a quarter mile away, without putting a mark on them. It was hard to get too mad at her. She was only taking the eggs we couldn't find. When her kittens had their fill, she would carry the rest up to the house and give them to us. Many were the times she would trot up to me and drop a perfect, unmarked egg at my feet. It was obvious that she included us in her responsibilities.

When everyone was fed for the morning, she would lie on the front porch and rest before her afternoon round of feeding everyone again. She always had time to wash some-one's face and ears or play with a kitten, even if it wasn't her own. She would lie quietly and switch the end of her tail for some little kitten to chase. Sometimes a little adventurous tom kitten wouldn't want to be bothered with having his face washed. Yolanda was more than able to deal with that problem. She would put her paw in the middle of his back and pin him against the porch floor. Then, while he squalled and squirmed, she would take her time and make sure every hair was clean and in place. You could almost hear the little guy complaining, *Aw, Mom, don't spit on your hankie and wipe my face in public.*

Yolanda always hid her kittens, bringing them out only when they were big enough to take care of themselves. Unfortunately, that meant that they ended up being half-wild little beasts. I only saw the tips of their tails as they disappeared into some deep, dark hiding place. It was different with her last litter, however.

I always stayed in the barn with my sows when they farrowed. Mama sows are terribly rough on their babies. The biggest losses in any litter come from the sows lying on the pigs. The second biggest losses come from bites from the mama. I found that if I stayed with the sows and delivered the pigs, I could save nearly twice as many pigs. I caught each pig as it was born and made sure each was dry and alert and steady on his feet. If a sow was inclined to attack her pigs, I would set up a washtub with a brooder lamp over it, and put the pigs into it as they were born. When she was finished, I cleaned the farrowing crate, gave her a drink, got her settled, and then put the pigs in one at a time. When I was sure all was well, I left them for the night.

It wasn't uncommon for two or three of our cats to keep me company when I was farrowing sows. So it was that night. I had three sows farrowing, and Yolanda was keeping me company. I would deliver a pig from each, and then have a moment to sit on the rail behind them before they started again. This was always one of my favorite things to do on the farm. The barn was dark and quiet, lit only by the brooder lamps in each crate. There were two or three litters already in some of the other crates, and some of the pigs were getting big enough that they would interact with you. If I hung over the side and talked to them, they would study my face and squeal and grunt. The barn was clean and everyone was fed and watered for the night. The sows I was farrowing were my own gentle, hand-raised pets, which made it easier. Unlike the first sows that we had bought, these would calm down if I spoke to them. Now all I had to do was bring one new life after another into the world. It was an an easy, companionable time. While I was sitting on the rail, waiting for the next pig to come along, Yolanda jumped into my lap and promptly dropped a wet little kitten in my lap. For the rest of the evening, after every third pig, I delivered a kitten and dried it off for her.

Yolanda lived six years, a long time for a barn cat. If I could have, I would have made her a pampered house cat with all the best care available, but I couldn't. I guess it doesn't really matter. Making her a pampered house pet would have made me happy, but she would have been miserable. Being outdoors, hunting, and caring for her extended family were what she loved; and I doubt she would have been happy being the center of attention herself. Besides, I couldn't have made her look any healthier than she did herself on her steady diet of eggs.

Of all the cats I have known since, I have never known another with such a generous spirit. She gave all the time and energy she had, every day, to making sure that others had what they needed. If I could but live up to her example, I know I would be a better person for it. I think the paper had it wrong: that cat and her descendants were not the best mousers in the county; they were the most generous cats in the county.

A Cat
Named Hope

Dee Sheppe

W hen my teenage son had his first major disappointment in life, I was at a loss to help him. Rob was a senior in high school, and he felt his future closing in on him. He had spent months and all his money making a film to apply to film school—and the film had been ruined during sound editing. His girlfriend, his brother, and I tried to talk to him, but he just sat for what seemed like hours with his head in his hands. Our cat, Hope, curled at his feet.

My son's trials made me think about Hope, how she had had such a difficult start in life and had grown into the most affectionate animal in the house. She greets me at the door when I come home. She sleeps on my bed. She's at peace with everybody and helped bring a calm and peacefulness to our house, which isn't easy when you've got two teenage sons, a couple of cats, and a dog.

To judge by our first meeting, I never would have guessed how much this cat would mean to our family. I'd seen her and her four kittens one day when I was volunteering at the local animal shelter. When I opened the cage to hold her, a staff member shouted a warning, "That cat is a terror!" But I saw that the mother cat was just scared in the crowded and noisy shelter and was determined to protect her babies.

Time was running out quickly on the mother and her kittens at the animal shelter. At the end of the day, I took the little family home, hoping I could foster them for a while and find them all homes later.

The mother cat was nervous and hostile in our house. When the kittens were ready, I brought the family back to the shelter for adoption. The kittens soon found good homes, but their mother wasn't so lucky—after a few days at the shelter, she got sick. I didn't know what it was about this cat, but I missed her. I took her home again from the shelter, figuring I'd nurse her back to health and put her back up for adoption. I still didn't even know her name.

But back at the shelter a third time, the mother cat, now healthy and adoptable, went ballistic! I had to get her out again. This time, I rushed to the veterinarian to have this "terror" spayed; I thought it would calm her down and make her more adoptable. I was so frustrated when I got her to the vet's that when the receptionist asked for the cat's name I blurted out, "I don't know! She's hopeless!"

Later, in the parking lot, it suddenly dawned on me. The cat had escaped the animal shelter not once, but three times. She'd beaten incredible odds and never gave up. Her name was obvious!

That afternoon we didn't even notice her near my son's feet. I held my breath as I watched Rob try to cope with his disappointment. At last, he stood up and stumbled, almost stepping on the cat. With a grin on his face he looked at us and said, "I almost stamped out Hope." The phrase became an inspiration in our household. Years later, we still use it on those days when we need encouragement. My son married his girl-friend, went on to film school, and became a successful television producer; and our wonderful cat is still with us. All of which proves that you can't stamp out Hope in this household.

Henrietta the Cat and Her Foreign Correspondent

Christopher S. Wren

Six months after I joined the *New York Times*, one of its two Moscow correspondents suddenly asked to return home for family reasons, well ahead of schedule. The editors looked around the newsroom for someone who spoke Russian, and saw me. Would I be at all interested?

Responding to this unanticipated miracle must have taken me all of three seconds. Once the shock subsided, I replied as calmly as I could, "How soon can I leave?"

The biggest problem I foresaw was our cat, Henrietta, because I didn't know how she would survive in strange new surroundings. She was playful enough with Celia and Chris. In fact, they had grown devoted to her.

But our cat had no visible street smarts. Her only travels outside our apartment had been in the back seat of our car to the cottage we rented in Putnam County, a couple of hours north of our Manhattan apartment. Even there, Jaqueline hesitated to let her out for fear of the local dogs or wilder predators, whom we suspected of having done in our previous cat.

198

One Saturday afternoon, Henrietta decided to climb a tree, and we spent the rest of the weekend coaxing her down.

"Don't be afraid," Jaqueline told the cat. "We'll catch you if you fall."

As a gesture of confidence, my soul mate added, "If Daddy misses, I'll drive you to the hospital."

Henrietta, pointed up but looking down, lost her grip and fell. Her claws deployed into my skull and shoulders. I pried her off and deposited her on the ground. She promptly dashed off and hid for a very long time under the porch, unhurt but definitely shaken.

In describing Henrietta back then, "spunky" and "intrepid" are not the sort of words that spring to mind. Her clumsy fall out of an uncomplicated tree did not augur well for a life behind the Iron Curtain.

It should be apparent by now that Henrietta and I didn't think much of each other, not at first. Henrietta sensed my fear that keeping her around would make it harder for me to succeed as a foreign correspondent.

To begin with, the cat would have to be given all kinds of expensive inoculations against rabies and more exotic diseases. She would need a traveling case heavy enough to withstand the tons of boxes and bags dumped on her by the baggage handlers. And for all its corporate benevolence, the *Times* refused to subsidize cats for its correspondents, so we would have to invest a tidy sum in Henrietta's travels.

Not least, I wondered whether my editors would consider

MORE STORIES OF CATS AND THE LIVES THEY TOUCH

it frivolous for a new reporter to venture onto the vast, windswept Russian steppes with cat in tow.

I invented all sorts of reasons for leaving Henrietta behind, as much for her sake as ours. I reminded Jaqueline that pets couldn't just rove hither and yon; many countries impose quarantine restrictions that our cat would not enjoy and might not survive. Another reporter I knew had to turn down a coveted assignment to our London bureau after his wife refused to submit their dog to the mandatory six-month quarantine in Britain; shortly thereafter, he quit the *Times*.

Over dinner one evening, I summoned up the courage to explain our dilemma to Chris and Celia, who by now had attained the prime listening ages of three and nearly seven years old.

Very soon we would be moving to a fairy-tale land called Russia, far, far away. And didn't Celia and Chris agree with me that Henrietta would be ever so much happier staying behind in New York City, where she had ever so many relatives?

And no—I anticipated the children's first question— taking all her relatives with us to Russia wasn't an option, because Henrietta couldn't tell us who they were or where they lived.

As the debate unfolded around our kitchen table, my mind was struggling to compile a short list of acquaintances who might consider taking the cat off our hands for two bottles of Scotch, or three at most.

Chris was not too young to sense that something here

was amiss. "But what about Henrietta?" he inquired suspiciously. Until now, he had let Celia do most of the talking.

I started to explain that our cat would have much more fun remaining in New York, but somewhere lovely and spacious, of course, maybe even Central Park. Then Celia interrupted me,

"Henrietta's going too," Celia assured her little brother.

"I'm not sure that's such a good—" I began.

Celia now addressed the cat in question, who at the time was more curious about what we were eating for dinner that she hadn't been allowed to sample first.

"Henrietta," Celia said, "you're going to live in Russia, aren't you?"

Henrietta perked up her ears at the prospect of foreign adventure.

Chris, beaming with relief, looked to his mother for reassurance. "Henrietta's going too?"

"How could we go anywhere without Henrietta?" Jaqueline assured our little boy. "Why, she'll even be riding right in the plane with us."

"I'll hold her all the way," Chris volunteered.

"We'll take turns," Celia said firmly.

The heart trumps the head every time. Henrietta went abroad because Celia and Chris could not conceive of living anywhere without her.

So the family cat who couldn't even find her way down from a tree was headed straight for the malevolent heart of the "Evil Empire," as Ronald Reagan later described the Soviet Union. And Henrietta didn't choose her fate; I did.

On an icy New Year's Eve, our cat, looking small and very frightened, flew from London into Moscow's Sheremetyevo International Airport, accompanying the foreign correspondent who didn't want her and his wife and two children who refused to leave the United States without her.

Entering the Soviet Union, we confronted a potentially serious problem: on New Year's Day, the *New York Times* would begin publishing excerpts from Aleksandr Solzhenitsyn's *The Gulag Archipelago*. My editors feared that once Solzhenitsyn's exposé of the Soviet penal system appeared, the Kremlin could retaliate by refusing to let me into the country. But if I was already sitting in the *Times's* Moscow bureau, the authorities would hesitate to throw me out, knowing that the American government would respond by expelling a Russian correspondent from Washington.

I worried that Henrietta would delay our arrival. To sneak in as inconspicuously as possible—my incognito entourage included only a beautiful wife, two lively, towheaded, English-speaking children, a couple of dozen pieces of luggage, and the family cat—we had chosen New Year's Eve, a holiday on which Russians are traditionally preoccupied with debauching themselves into collective oblivion.

The biting winter cold sent Henrietta into shivers as her travel cage was trundled past snowdrifts bordering the slick tarmac. Sheremetyevo's arrivals terminal reeked of wet woolen overcoats, chlorine disinfectant, coarse cigarettes, and other pungent odors. They warned her that this destination was neither familiar nor hospitable.

Suspicious border guards with bayonets fixed on their Kalashnikov assault rifles scrutinized the stream of passengers as we milled past. The customs officials watched Henrietta's travel cage being dumped on the grimy inspection counter. They resented having to work on New Year's Eve, which more fortunate Russians were celebrating with sentimental toasts.

A gray-jacketed customs officer looked us over and then saw the cat cage.

"*Skoro budyet,*" he said. It will happen soon.

"What will be soon?" I asked.

"You brought an animal with you," he said. "The veterinary inspection will happen soon."

"Soon" turned out to be more than a half hour until the veterinarian on duty finally showed up. She was a stout woman wearing a long, white lab coat and exhibiting the surliness of the Soviet bureaucracy. It was up to her to decide whether the trembling contents of Henrietta's cage deserved admittance to the Union of Soviet Socialist Republics or should be packed off to some quarantine confines with all the comforts of a Siberian salt mine.

The veterinarian frowned at the untranslated English of the cat's vaccination papers, which she obviously could not read. A *nyet* from her would leave us mired in the

Soviet bureaucracy long after our window of opportunity had passed. I started to panic.

But as I silently reproached myself for putting my job in jeopardy by dragging a cat to my first foreign assignment, the vet pulled Henrietta out of her cage, but gently, and her official brusqueness melted away.

"*Kakaya krasivaya Amerikanskaya koshka!*" marveled the veterinarian. What a beautiful little American cat!

An American cat? The rest of attendant Soviet official-dom jostled in for a look. Peering up, Henrietta greeted them with a plaintive meow that seemed to plead, *Will you get me out of here?*

Laughter replaced the sullen silence as the officials took turns petting the American cat—yes, my Henrietta.

"*Koshka ustala.*" The cat must be tired traveling all the way from America, someone observed. In fact, we had stopped over in London, where Henrietta had had to spend a couple of nights in the quarantine facility near London's Heathrow International Airport. More likely, she desperately needed to find a litter box.

And the yawning American children, someone else said. "*Malyshi ustali tozhe.*" The kids look tired too.

For Henrietta's sake we were rushed through the remaining formalities faster than I've ever cleared a Russian airport on scores of flights. No longer was anyone concerned about how much money we were carrying or what kind of subversive literature we might have stashed in the linings of our suitcases. Whatever ideological distaste the Russian officials were obliged to display toward decadent Americans exempted Henrietta, a cat who would look at home on any Russian hearth.

Far from slowing us up, Henrietta had interceded to get us into the country. We were asleep, with the cat curled up on one of the children's beds in our new apartment over-looking Moscow's Ring Road, by the time Solzhenitsyn's denunciation of the country that had just admitted us appeared on the *Times*'s front page.

I monitored Henrietta's activities in Moscow when I caught sight of her from the window over my desk in the *Times* bureau. Or, going out to drive the bureau car to an inter-view, I'd watch her sitting and staring at a potential mouse hole in some wall down the street, or maybe stalking the occasional bird. Or a neighbor in our compound would call out, "Say, wasn't that your cat I saw down at the Uzbekistan Restaurant? Don't you feed her enough?"

I had assumed that our cat was pretty much useless beyond her entertainment value for Celia and Chris. It did not take long for Henrietta to prove me wrong.

One evening, I came home from the *Times* bureau for dinner to find Jaqueline in an agitated state. "You've got to do something about Henrietta," she said.

I was tempted to say, "I'll book her on the next Aeroflot flight back to New York." But I held my tongue. My wife led me into the living room, where we encountered Henrietta suspended halfway to the ceiling like some levitating swami.

To be more accurate, the cat had clawed her way up the bright curtains and was dangling inches below a *mysha*—a small Russian mouse—whose palpable fear had overcome the natural forces of gravity. Before I could step in, Henrietta lunged upward to seize the mouse's tail in her teeth, executed an incredible backflip in midair, and landed four-footed on the carpet with her wriggling prey.

I was dazzled. Our clumsy New York kitten had just demonstrated her dexterity at a skill that would make her indispensible to our years abroad. And if the denouement of the chase turned somewhat bloody, well, Lenin had warned us that a cat wearing gloves catches no mice. Or was that Benjamin Franklin?

By now Henrietta was no mere pet but an active member of our family. Yet it embarrassed me to admit that she remained more skittish of me than of many Russians she had met, realizing perhaps that I had opposed bringing her to Moscow. This subtle estrangement ended abruptly one Sunday in September, after I was assaulted while covering an art show.

I had gone off to Moscow's southwestern outskirts to see an unofficial exhibition of dissident art set up in an empty lot near the Belyayevo subway station. I was talking with some artists when a bunch of husky strangers, who turned out to be Soviet cops in civilian clothes, arrived and set about breaking up the exhibition, quite literally. One man driving a bulldozer knocked over the paintings. His colleagues fed some canvases into a bonfire they had built. The artists who protested or stood their ground were roughed up or taken away to the local precinct.

I tried to take a photograph of the unprovoked attack and had my Nikon camera slammed into my teeth. Then, while two plainclothes thugs pinned my arms behind my back, a third thug slammed his beefy fist into my stomach just below the belt.

I returned home with a story to write, but the truth is that I didn't feel much like writing it. One of my front teeth was chipped, and the rest of my mouth ached. My stomach hurt too. There was no point calling the police; my assailants had been the police. When I telephoned the doctor at the American Embassy, he said that unless I had blood in my urine, the assault sounded like something that would not require his professional services.

Jaqueline was worried, of course. "You ought to lie down," she said. "We'll go to Helsinki to have Dr. Gran"— our Finnish dentist—"fix your teeth."

I protested that I had to write my eyewitness account of the senseless demolition of the art exhibit. But I followed my solicitous wife's orders, and she agreed to wake me in an hour.

Of course, I couldn't sleep. I lay across our double bed feeling as sorry for myself as for the artists who had had their safety as well as their art violated. I wondered whether to send a message to the foreign desk that I was too banged up from the assault to file myself, and ask them to run an account from the wire agencies.

And then I felt something hop softly on the bed. I opened my eyes and saw Henrietta creeping up silently alongside me. She liked to curl up with the children and Jaqueline but had never seen fit to favor me with such a visit.

I shut my eyes again and felt Henrietta rub against my leg and nestle down against my hip. Then I heard her purr.

I reached down and lightly caressed the soft fur along her neck. She snuggled in tighter until my sore mouth and gut no longer throbbed. There is something consoling about stroking a pet when you feel frightened and alone. For the first time, it was clear that Henrietta and I belonged together.

Her purring continued for some time, reminding me over and over, "Don't let human nature get you down."

After a while, Henrietta got up and sprang off the bed. *She's right,* I thought, *we've both got better things to do.* I walked across the courtyard to the office, sat down, and wrote my account of the destruction of the art exhibit. The *Times* featured it across the front page the next morning and later flew me to Helsinki to get my teeth fixed.

What more can I say, except that thereafter Henrietta and I got along famously?